What Does It Mean to Be a Man?

What Does It Mean to Be a Man?

THOMAS HART

Paulist Press
New York/Mahwah, N.J.

Book design by Lynn Else
Cover design by Trudi Gershenov

Library of Congress Cataloging-in-Publication Data

Hart, Thomas N.
What does it mean to be a man? / Thomas Hart.
p. cm.
ISBN 0-8091-4167-1 (alk. paper)
1. Man (Theology) I. Title.

BT701.3.H37 2004
248.8'42—dc22

2004006022

Published by Paulist Press
997 Macarthur Boulevard
Mahwah, New Jersey 07430

www.paulistpress.com

Printed and bound in the
United States of America

CONTENTS

INTRODUCTION

On a recent summer night in Tacoma, Washington, a city 30 miles south of Seattle, a 30-year-old man walking home from work was beaten to death by a group of seven boys—one 11, two 12, one 14, two 15, and one 19. They were not a gang, and the man, who had walked the same route home every day for years, was a complete stranger to them. "Want to get him?" the 19-year-old asked the group. They got him, all right. They approached, and one asked him for a cigarette while another came alongside him and slugged him in the face. Then they all kicked, stomped, and punched him, while the 11-year-old beat him with a stick. If he tried to rise, they "knee-dropped" him—twenty-eight times. When they were done, they walked away. Their motive? "They did it for the excitement and entertainment it provided them," the prosecutor's office reported. When the story hit the Seattle papers, eight copycat attacks were made on men walking alone in Seattle the following night.

Is this what it means to be a man?

An incident like this shocks and horrifies all of us. Yet it is not totally unfamiliar. That is because teen violence, guns in school, vandalism, drug and alcohol abuse, and gang activity have established themselves as elements of the urban landscape. The same is true for sexual harassment, date rape, fraternity gang rape, and sadistic hazing on college campuses. We hate hearing of such things. We push it aside, hoping we have heard the last of it. But then it happens again. What might be driving this kind of behavior?

Some say, "That is just the way young people are today." But if we look closely, we can be more specific. It is not young girls who are doing these things. Girls have their own problems, but with rare exceptions they do not engage in actions like these. This is young boy behavior. And it does not take too much rumination to realize that in these bizarre ways, boys are trying to prove that they are men.

In his book *The Eight Masks of Men,* Frederick Grosse, a minister who has worked extensively with adult men's groups, observes that most men are lonely, most men are angry, and most men are wearing masks. Those are strong statements, but, having counseled men for thirty-five years myself, I find a lot of truth in them. And I discern a line of continuity between some of the ways boys act out and the way men often turn out.

We come to male adulthood conditioned to be tough. We view other men competitively and jockey for dominance even when it is unnecessary and inappropriate. We have learned to hide the softer parts of our humanity, and now have difficulty feeling or expressing those parts even when we want to. We can easily be sexual without real love or concern. We slip quite readily into anger and violence. We do not know how to make friends with other men even when there is desire on both sides. We struggle to relate to our spouses and children sensitively or in depth.

But our plight is far from hopeless.

First, our conditioning has helped us develop many strengths. We can withstand hardship and pain. We are self-reliant and usually calm in the face of challenge or danger. We know how to express love by doing things for others. We take our role as breadwinners seriously and work hard for our families. We are problem solvers. We play to win generally. We are assertive, adept at looking after our interests and those of the people we love. We lead with relative ease. We are not afraid to take risks. These are all wonderful assets.

We are also increasingly aware of our deficits and are working to become more whole. Many of us today are more developed emotionally, have made progress in our capacity for interpersonal intimacy, and are better partners to the women we love. Older models of macho manhood are losing their appeal, and we are working harder at developing our too-long-neglected inner selves. Though we have a ways to go, we are better at all these things than we used to be, even a generation ago.

I write this book in the hopes of assisting that development still further. Most of us would probably admit that we could still use some help recovering and expanding our life of feeling. We would like to enjoy greater emotional intimacy with the people we love, and are not always sure how to go about it. We wish we could manage our anger better and not move so quickly toward violence, even verbal violence. We would like to control our sexuality rather than watch it control us, and integrate it into mature loving. We would like to find, and then to hold, a special person to live our lives with, be best friends with, and share the responsibilities of home and family as real partners. We wish we could be not just providers but good fathers to our children, enjoying close relationships with them. We want to find our niche in the world of work and to make our contribution. At some level, perhaps we even long to be in harmony with the deeper energies of the universe, in alignment with whatever made us, and enjoy the benefits of a spiritual life.

But how do we do all this?

In my work of counseling men (and women) as spiritual guide and psychotherapist, I have observed what makes men tick, what our typical struggles are, and what helps us move through narrow defiles and rocky places into fertile plains. I have looked deeply into our relationships with women and with other men. And I have watched families. All this while, I have worked at my own personal growth, for a long time as a celibate person in religious life, then as a married man. Both by study and by rich personal encounters, I have learned a lot about psychology and spirituality. From both wells I drink deeply and would like to share what I have found. If life is a baseball game, I am in the last of the seventh inning. It is from there that I write, speaking of some of the lessons that the great game has taught me.

My concern is not just the individual man and his immediate circle, but the larger world in which we live. That world needs healing badly. And we men wield a lot of power in its past and future shaping. Perhaps if we worked at our own growth as persons and became healthier and more whole, we would see and address the chronic problems of war, hunger, disease, and poverty in a quite different way. We might create a more just economy. We might be gentler with the Earth, the ecosystem within which we and our children will live for generations to come.

I see severe limitations, both for the individual and for the universe, in the macho model of manhood. But I have no interest in developing soft men. My goal is whole men. The Table of Contents catalogues all the areas on which we need to reflect. At the end of the book I offer discussion questions for men's groups, because these groups can be such a fertile context for our growth. The questions can also be used for personal reflection.

I come to our conversation with a conviction and a dream. My conviction is that if we were willing to work at achieving the fullness of our humanity, we would find our lives much richer and far more satisfying. My dream is of how this personal development, moving across the landscape, could gradually transform the world.

1

HEALING BOYHOOD WOUNDS

The trouble begins when a little boy is told that boys don't cry. How old is he? Three or four, perhaps, five at most. It is probably Dad who tells him, or it may be an older brother. The message is often not given very kindly. "Sissy." "Crybaby." "What's the matter with you? Are you a girl?" This is a moment of immense developmental consequence. From the moment he was born, this little kid has cried every time he felt pain or had some need. His crying instinct is no different from that of his sister, a purely natural response. And up to this point, it has usually gotten a helpful response: Someone has come to his aid. Now, suddenly, this same spontaneous expression of distress is condemned. It is not masculine. The boy's gender education has begun.

What is a boy to do? If he wants to avoid being shamed by the males who surround him, there is only one thing he can do. He learns to hide his feelings. He pretends that sadness, fear, need are no longer any part of his experience. He learns to be stoic, to put on a poker face no matter what may be coming at him. Look tough. Seem to be in control. Betray not the slightest sign of the turmoil, confusion, pain inside, for these things are not masculine.

Soon the boy is out among other boys. They have been similarly conditioned and will assist him with his training. They will harden him further, and soon he will be involved in hardening other boys. "Sissy," "weakling," "wimp," "wuss," "faggot," "chicken," "chickenshit" will be freely flung at anyone who flinches. There will be fights, endurance contests, and dares to prove oneself a man. From my own boyhood, I remember what we called "six-inch fights." Two of us would square off, and with closed fist take turns hitting each other in the upper arm from six inches away, until one of us (the weakling) said, "OK, that's enough." Our upper arms would be black and blue for a week. There were other contests to determine who would flinch first, an obvious sign of being chicken. The boy who shows himself toughest emerges as the leader, because he is most feared by the others, and also offers the first line of defense against enemies. But what sort of boy is being formed? One man looks back on his childhood.

> In the third grade, I was in an argument with another boy that led to some pushing and shouting. Suddenly, certainly without my ever expecting it, he swung and hit me in the face with his closed fist. I cried. I think some of the tears must have been on account of having to give up the reassuring illusion that all boys played by my family's unstated code (we wrestled, but never hit one another, certainly not in the face). I learned the more universal code of the schoolyard. Boys don't cry. Boys don't walk away from fights. And if you do either, you're chicken, a sissy, or queer.

Where does this lead? Franklin Abbott, who writes on what it means to be a man, summarizes it this way.

> America has a boy problem. Unfortunately, this "boy problem" remains relatively invisible. We know it as something else: teen violence, urban gangs, guns in school, elementary school sexual harassment, suburban

violence, fraternity gang rape. Just who, exactly, is doing it? Girls? These are boys desperate to prove something, to show they are real men. Because in this culture, being a real man is vital to every boy.

Passing On the Sting

How does "getting gendered" play out a bit later in a boy's life? Join a fraternity, and you will get hazed. The ordeals are notched up now, so you will have ample opportunity to prove your masculine endurance. At the University of Washington a couple of years ago, a young man committed suicide after his hazing. We can only speculate why, as he left no account. Did he feel that he did not quite measure up to the male standard, even though he had survived the ordeals? Or did he feel that if this is the male world, he wanted no part of it?

If you join the military, you will get toughened up even more, bullied so that you learn to bully, violently dealt with so that you learn to be violent. The intention there is to make you tough enough to kill, sometimes also to torture. It is a process of brutalizing and dehumanizing a recruit until the desired product is produced.

Psychotherapist and college professor Gordon Murray reflects on the Gulf War. He says that he was totally opposed to the war, yet felt a certain dark but familiar satisfaction in picking on the little guy, remembering how good it feels to beat someone up. He calls this behavior "passing on the sting," which means finding someone weaker than yourself on whom to inflict the pain that someone stronger once inflicted on you. His reflection then takes him back a few years to the Vietnam War and Lyndon Johnson's remarks after he ordered the first bombing of North Vietnam: "I didn't just screw Ho Chi Minh, I cut his pecker off." Of a member of his Administration who was becoming doubtful of the war, Johnson said, "Hell, he has to squat to piss." Yes, Johnson was a plain-talking Texan, but the fact that the president of the United States can say such things reveals quite a bit about notions of manhood in America. It is tough, and bears no taint of the feminine.

> As I thought about the sting, I remembered a particularly brutal murder here in San Francisco a while back. In this case, the sting was passed on quickly. A gay man in his fifties named Smoot was found murdered in his apartment. Nothing was stolen; the motive must have been something less obvious than need or greed. They found the culprit, a young man. He claimed in his defense that Smoot had made unwelcome sexual advances towards him. As his story unfolded, it turned out that not long before he murdered Smoot, a group of the young man's peers had raped him with a broom handle.

In boyhood, passing on the sting is usually less severe, but perhaps no easier for a child to bear. Who can guess the inner agonies of those targeted? Today's school shootings, a desperate striking back, sometimes spell it out for us.

> Marco was the unofficial scapegoat for our after-school group. He was weird-looking, wore glasses, was fat and hyper, did gross things, talked a lot of Spanish, and was tough enough to survive all the abuse we dealt him. Basically, whenever we wanted to make fun of, hurt, or trick someone, we picked Marco.

Take your average grown man, conditioned by these processes. He has learned to hide all that his male peers regard as unmanly: his pain, sadness, fear, loneliness, need, possibly even his tender affection. He has been taught to believe that it is not OK to express any of these undeniably significant parts of his emotional life. What is the consequence? He is wearing a mask. He is lonely. He is angry. And socially, he is boring. He puts out very little with which to connect. And he does not know how to connect. He has very little to say. When he does speak, he talks almost entirely of outer events. How he feels in relation to outer events is no part of his report. He can show certain emotions that are acceptably masculine: anger, sarcasm, aggressiveness, contempt. But such a diet does not make for an interesting afternoon or evening together. No wonder men usually prefer the company of women. The spontaneity of a woman's feelings and the richness of her inner life have not been worked over by violent hands.

But our conditioned man's plight may be sorrier yet. He may believe that it is not all right even to *feel* half the human feelings if he is really a man, so he begins to push them out of his awareness. After some years of this, he cannot even find these feelings inside. Ask him as a friend or spouse what he is feeling in very emotional situations, and he will look at you blankly. He does not know. He cannot locate anything. As a therapist, I remember a particular young man who was almost totally cut off from his feelings. I asked him one time, "When you are alone in a room, who is there?" And he said, "No one." It reminded me of what a therapist friend once remarked to me: "Loneliness is 80 percent loneliness for one's self. There is no one inside."

So men go out to watch women dance topless. How fascinated we are by that wonderful beauty, softness, and warmth. How we hunger for that, so little of which abides in our bleak world. The problem is, we cannot access that by merely watching. Even a sexual encounter, if we could get it, would not reach the hurting place in us, would it?

Would it ever occur to us in watching nude women dance that they represent the buried parts of ourselves? In other words, that we too are soft, warm, and beautiful, but that we have been sold a bill of goods and strictly forbidden to develop this whole dimension of ourselves. Can we express any of the inner pain of our lives to another person, man or woman? Now that would really help. It would represent a return to the truth of our existence. It would also be a movement toward true intimacy, genuine closeness. Risky, yes. Unmanly too by a certain standard. It breaks the rule. And yet what a relief. There must be some confirmation of the rightness of the action just by that feeling of relief.

Raising Our Sons

If we are going to end with a different kind of man, we have to start with the boy. And we must begin by *not* doing something. We have to tear up, burn, and bury that age-old adage that turns spontaneous boys into truncated men: "Boys don't cry." Real boys do cry. Real men do too. If they cannot, they are not real at all. They still have their masks on.

The key figure in a boy's formation is his dad. A boy will tend to identify with his same sex parent, and will learn countless unspoken lessons from him. He will also learn what Dad teaches him in dialogue—if Dad is willing to spend time with him and talk with him about things that are important.

That is just where the problem often begins. Dads often fail to spend much time with their sons, or spend it in shared activities but without substantive communication. A whole chapter on fathering comes later in this book. But we might briefly consider an issue or two here.

If we do spend time with our sons and lead the way into deeper communication, we can begin by naming and celebrating with them all that is good about being male: physical strength and endurance, the ability to defend ourselves and to come to the rescue of the defenseless, clearheadedness, male camaraderie and competitiveness, our desire to bond with and enjoy the feminine and to be providers. We can also make them aware of how some of our male traits can lead us down wrong roads. A good defense can turn into a very offensive offense, mere bullying. Competitiveness can become ruthless and unethical, our whole lives organized around winning. We can allow our sex drive to be exploitive and destructive, disrespectful of others as persons. We can be strongly rational, but barren emotionally. In fact, we can neglect the development of our inner life entirely and be hollow shells. Camaraderie can be mere superficiality, the best we can do at interpersonal relationships.

Our sons need particular guidance as they enter the rough world of other boys and begin to receive the messages that destroy their capacity to feel, to share feelings, and to be genuine. How can we teach them that it is fine to be tough, but that they must never lose their capacity to be soft and vulnerable too, depending on circumstances. What if a father, who most likely already appears very strong to his son, were to share some of the less conspicuous parts of his emotional experience, to admit to his son that he felt sad sometimes, that some things frightened him, that he was familiar with loneliness, that at times he felt like giving up? What if he let his son see him cry? What if he apologized to his son when he knew he had wronged him, even if it was only by neglect? Would he lose stature in his son's eyes? Or would his son learn that the entire range of his own feelings was OK and was destined to persist into healthy male adulthood? To be able to do this, a father might have to do some personal remedial work, against his own conditioning, to become more comfortable with the full range of his own emotions. To this important project we devote the next chapter.

I recently concluded a counseling relationship with a man in his thirties. He was a gentle man, married, with a daughter and a son. Ours was a mentoring relationship, a monthly session in which we talked about many different issues, our focus usually arising out of whatever concerns or questions the last few weeks had raised for him. One day, after two or three years of this, he told me that he thought he was finished. I asked him how he knew that. He said that he had just gone to visit the father of a boy who was bullying his son. They had worked the problem through successfully, and he felt very good about it. The encounter told him that he was a lot healthier, because it had taken courage to go meet that man and talk about this problem. He did not know what sort of response he might get. But he loved his son, who had a physical handicap, and he wanted the bullying to stop. I appreciated his personal victory, as well as the strategy he had chosen for helping his son. He could hardly ask his son to go beat up someone older and stronger than himself. He might have gone to school authorities or the police. Had he met and threatened the boy with consequences if the behavior continued, would that not be just more of the same—the stronger using threats on the weaker? Would anybody learn anything? So what he chose to do was to see if he could convert the boy's father to nonviolence—or perhaps he found him already converted, I do not remember. And he occasioned a teaching moment between that father and his son. He had shown both boys, and another man, that he could be both strong and gentle.

One thing we know from our adult experience, which our sons do not, is that the adult world does not play by quite the same rules as the world of boys. The boy who is physically weaker might be very successful later, when the competition is no longer quite so physical. The boy who has empathy and deals sensitively with other individuals might be a great success in business or the professions. The boy who is artistic or intuitive might be a peripheral figure in the competitions of boys, but make a significant contribution later to human society. A man can affirm all the varied strengths and abilities in his sons when peers are not affirming them at all. Someday, as men, these "lesser" boys might help their more robust peers to a truer humanity.

Reading Suggestions

Franklin Abbott edits a rich collection of stories of growing up male in his *Boyhood: Growing Up Male* (Madison, WI: University of Wisconsin Press, 1993). They can help us remember buried aspects of our own growing up, and serve as a stimulus for discussion of the issues in men's groups. All three of the quoted recollections in this chapter, as well as Abbott's own description of our "boy problem" are from this book (pp. ix, 31, 34, 49).

Joe Kita, in his *The Wisdom of Our Fathers* (Emmaus, PA: Rodale Press, 1999), compiles the thoughts of 138 wise old dads on such topics as growing old and staying young; work, money, and success; sex, women, and love; fatherhood, death, difficulty, and despair; and the key to happiness. What prompted Kita to undertake the project is that fathers so seldom pass on their wisdom to their sons. His own father had not. So Kita gathers the wisdom he can find and passes it on in book form to all the sons who never get it from their dads. It is a delightful read.

A recent film, *Boys Don't Cry,* depicts the male culture of cruelty with unforgettable poignancy.

2

RECOVERING YOUR WORLD OF FEELING

I asked a fellow therapist and good friend what I should talk about in my book for men. "Above all," he said, "men need permission to feel. Invite and encourage them to feel. That will begin to change their lives."

Women's most common complaint about the men they love is that they do not share themselves, and, when you come right down to it, are pretty boring a lot of the time. They put out very little to relate to. Yesterday a woman client suddenly burst out:

> Why do men build walls? What are they so afraid of? All Mike wants to do when he comes home from work is drink beer and watch TV. He says he's tired. I'm tired too, but I certainly don't want to do that!

I want to suggest that there is a problem behind men's silence. It is that we have very little to communicate, except in the realm of the practical. And that is because of the poverty of our inner lives. The core of the problem is that we have shunted off many of our human feelings. And that started back in boyhood, as we saw earlier. What a man needs to do, if he wants to come back to life, is to recover the full range of his feelings. That takes some hard work. But it starts with a permission. Can a man feel the full range of human emotions and still be a man?

Permission to Feel

Men usually feel and are free to express certain emotions: their anger, cynicism, enthusiasm for sports, attraction to women. These feelings are widely taken for "masculine," and are therefore socially acceptable. But there are a host of other feelings inside us that we hide from others, and often even from ourselves. I mean our sadness, fears, self-doubt, embarrassment or shame, inadequacy (we *know* we're boring), longings, regrets, quandaries, needs, empathy for others. To take the single instance of our needs, many a man thinks his mate should just *know* his needs without his saying anything, so, if she fails to guess and meet them, he gives her the sting of his anger. But he finds it hard to ask for what he needs or wants.

What about this larger world of feelings, though? Are we even in touch with them? Could we name what we feel in various situations if we wanted to? Or have we learned to push many of our feelings so far down that we can no longer find them? This is probably a man's sorriest state, a case of disowned and forgotten parts, and a sadly truncated remainder.

But even if we do feel and could name all these softer, sometimes embarrassing human emotions moving about inside us, would we have the courage to share them? Can a man admit to these feelings and still be a man? For many, that is the question. What do *you* think? It all hinges on whether you buy the idea that men are supposed to cultivate just a partial set of the human qualities, and women another partial set, or whether you believe that all the human qualities are both possible and desirable for persons of both sexes to cultivate, display, and enjoy.

I strongly believe in the latter principle. I appeal to experience. A woman who, in addition to being sensitive, gentle, empathic, and nurturing, is able to think clearly, solve problems, show the energy of her anger, and exercise leadership, is a far more interesting woman, and enjoys a much richer life, than her less developed peers. And a man who, in addition to being a capable thinker, problem solver, money earner, and leader, is also able to be gentle, nurturing, deep, empathic, and expressive, is a far more interesting man, and enjoys a much richer life, than his less developed peers. And such men and women in combination make excellent collaborators, friends, and lovers. On both sides, there is so much more to relate to, be challenged by, and enjoy.

Why do men generally find a deeper satisfaction in the company of women than in that of other men, even when there is no sex involved? Because women are by and large much more interesting *as persons.* They freely share more of their inner selves, and there is a lot going on inside of them. They usually exhibit warmth, a genuine interest, and a desire to relate person to person. Even women, though they are attracted to men, often find greater satisfaction in the company of women, and will usually count another woman as their best friend even when they are married. Why? Because women share emotional intimacy with other women, the same thing they offer men. So they bond with one another and become real friends. Men much more typically share activities with one another rather than intimacies, and often remain relative strangers to each other at deeper levels. We know something of another person when we know their interests and their ideas. But we hardly know them personally until they start telling us how they feel about various things.

This, then, is the best case I can make for your working to recover, develop, and share your inner self: It will give you more life. Do you want quality of life, a fully rounded personality, satisfying relationships with your mate, your children, and your friends? Do you want love in your life? It is hard to imagine a person who does not. Well, recovering your world of feeling and sharing more of it with others is the only road that goes there.

Coming Back to Life

If you are in this hefty group of men who cannot feel much and are afraid to express what they do feel because it is not "masculine," what do you do to exit your predicament?

First, you have to say that you are ready to revise your previous notion of what it means to be a man. You have seen through it, and you do not buy it. You are tired of being lonely and angry and wearing a mask, tired of your inadequacy in many social situations and your superficiality even in your better relationships. You want to be more of a human being.

Then you have to reestablish contact with your feelings. You have to let them up from the cellar into the living room and be hospitable to them, even the ones you do not like. "I am feeling sad." Feel it. "I am lonely." Sit with it. "I feel inferior to those around me, or inadequate to this situation." Feel it. Ask your feelings to come to you so you can experience them. When a feeling comes, thank it and feel it in your body. Thus, you will begin to establish a livelier relationship with your whole inner world. It is part of you, and you must embrace all that belongs to you if you would be whole.

Many feelings have a physical component, and you can get in touch with your feelings by getting more in touch with your body. Sexual desire has a familiar resonance in your loins. Embarrassment sometimes brings a blush to your face or ears. Fear or anxiety might cause you to perspire, or might tighten your stomach muscles. Anger might tighten your shoulder muscles, or get you breathing harder; or it might constrict your throat. Sadness feels heavy, and might make you droop; it also takes energy away. So if it is hard to bring feelings to awareness as feelings, you might begin just by paying attention to these physiological changes in your body as clues to the stirring of your emotions.

In this effort to recover your lost emotional life, it is more important to feel than to be able to name what you are feeling.

Sometimes you will not know exactly what it is, only that something is moving in you. Acknowledging that and giving it its space and time is the main thing. But then see if you can possibly identify it. There are four main feelings: sad, mad, glad, and scared. Check your feeling against each of these for a match. Finer shadings can come later. You can also get a lead from the situation. After what just happened, what would I (or somebody else) be likely to feel? That is probably what I am feeling. Now let me see if I can become aware of that in my body and spirit.

To get in better touch with my own feelings, I regularly use a technique I learned from psychologist Eugene Gendlin, which he calls "focusing." When I notice that I am feeling unpeaceful and am not sure why, I sit and close my eyes and go inside just to be with whatever is going on there. Gendlin compares it to taking a hurting child on your lap and asking, "Tell me, what's the matter?" I just sit with it and listen to it. I do not go up into my head to try to analyze it. This is not head, but gut, work. I stay in my belly, where the feeling usually is, and invite it to speak to me, even to name itself. And it usually does. It might give me a single adjective, such as "overwhelmed," "sad," "hurt," "exhausted." Or an image, such as "I feel as if I'm climbing and climbing and climbing and never reaching the top of the hill," or "I feel as if there are hands around my neck choking me." My experience is that whenever I just sit with a feeling like this and let it speak, listen to it with care, I already feel relief, even if my situation in life changes not at all. Gendlin's focusing is an instance of that attitude of interest and welcome, which invites all of our feelings to be at home in us and give up their information. A friend once called our emotions an elaborate communication system telling us how we are in the world.

There are some other techniques besides focusing that can help us get in touch with our feelings. Journaling can be very helpful, especially if it is focused particularly on the feelings we have in relation to the events we write about. There are men's groups, or sometimes just one well-chosen man, with whom we can find and share the feelings inside us. And there is individual therapy, that regular meeting with another person, male or female, with whom we share ourselves more and more fully, answering questions that take us to deeper places, and getting feedback that leads to still fuller self-awareness.

When the poet Robert Bly, a leader in the men's movement, was interviewed several years ago by Bill Moyers, he talked about this problem of men being out of touch with their feelings. And he offered a key to the lock. He said that he thought the way into that hidden realm for many men was to come back to their relationship with their father, and grieve it. Most men have sadness about that relationship. Whether he was physically or verbally abusive, too demanding or controlling, or just not there very much, Dad failed to give a lot of sons what they needed: personal interest, affirmation, and the conferring of a sense of what it means to be a man. Many a boy is pained to realize that he never learned who his father was, and now the chance is gone. This is the grief Bly is referring to, this mix of sadness and anger over what might have been and never was, which leaves a son thrust into the world to make his way alone. Bly's insight is that if that son can get in touch with the feelings he has about that, it will help him get in touch with his whole world of emotions.

The feeling many men are most comfortable exhibiting, anger, can be another doorway into the larger realm of our feelings. For hidden beneath our hard anger there often lies one of three more tender feelings: hurt, sadness, or fear.

If a man believes that hurt feelings are unacceptable in a real man, he carefully hides his hurt and just gives us the benefit of his anger. His wife says something to him, and instead of saying, "That hurt my feelings," he cuts her down. Now her feelings are hurt, and she will either attack back or pull away. The exchange would play out very differently if he said that her remark had hurt his feelings. She would probably stop short, surprised and concerned, and the damage would end there. But a man has to be willing to share his hurt. It is hard for him to do, by the old male rules, because he is admitting that he is (oh, no!) vulnerable. But it is the truth, and he knows it.

Similarly, "I am feeling sad today," sure beats putting a fist through the wall, kicking an animal, or being silent all day. Our mate or friend or child would be interested to hear about that and might even comfort us. It is not at all interesting to see or hear a fit of anger.

Fear is the third feeling that often lies under anger, in some ways the most surprising of them to choose that mode of expression. But it does. When we feel threatened, suddenly insecure, there is an instinctive rush of anger. It is the self-defense energy that expresses itself in the fight-or-flight response planted in all animals, ourselves included. This is the energy that makes conservatives lash out at liberals, who threaten their worldview and even their world. It is what makes insecure heterosexuals lash out at homosexuals, for the same reason. It is often at work on a smaller scale in the home, when our mate says something that threatens our sense of self or our position. Anger flashes. When that happens in you, look for the fear, and, if you have the courage, tell her about that, and you will probably have a fruitful discussion. Show her your anger only, and neither of you will learn anything.

So another key for you if you wish to recover your world of feelings is to become curious about your anger and look beneath it for what is generating this energy. Is it hurt, sadness, or fear? If you can identify and acknowledge one of these, and if you are willing to share that feeling instead of just showing anger, you will promote intimacy instead of killing it. You will know yourself better, and have important information to share so others can understand you too.

The Courage to Let Yourself Be Known

If the first step in your reclamation project is to feel and name your feelings, the second is to share them—not with everyone, for that would not be wise, but in relationships where you feel safe and would like to be closer. If the first task requires the virtue of patience and will deepen your humility, the second demands courage.

Can you begin to say to someone you trust the sorts of things we just looked at: "I was hurt." "I feel sad, and I could use a hug." "I really should talk to my boss, but I think I'm afraid of him." "I'm sorry" (i.e., I feel ashamed of what I did, and sad about the hurt I caused you). It takes a lot of courage, doesn't it? Can you cry? You cried freely and spontaneously as a little boy. Real men can be profoundly grieved by personal loss, touched by unexpected kindness, shaken by trauma. We have all seen photos of the bravest and toughest—young men at war—dissolving in tears in a comrade's arms at the horror of it all. But should it take that much tragedy for a man to cry? Many a man has told me that he wishes he could cry. He is full of tears, but has built such a dam against them that they cannot get through. He longs for release, but his conditioning will not yield.

So the work we are looking at is slow, progress gradual. Sometimes you succeed. And then you fail again, falling into the same old habits. That is very normal in a change process. In baseball, the very best hitters hit .300. That means they fail 70 percent of the time, often with men on base, and quietly sit down again until their next at bat. For many a man, to feel again, and to share his feelings, is as difficult as hitting a line drive. Be patient. Celebrate even a small success as a breakthrough, because it is those first slight alterations that are hardest to achieve, but which signal a turning of the corner and the start of a new direction. Begin by picking relatively safe people, and sharing some of your tenderer feelings with them. Push yourself a little, out of your comfort zone, into a space where you feel vulnerable (scared), sometimes even naked. You will be surprised to find out that the person not only does not despise you, as you feared, but values your sharing, understands it, respects it, and is often moved to match it with personal disclosures of his or her own.

That happened to me when I was twenty-one. I was a very self-controlled young man, and felt that I had earned the respect of my peers in the areas of my strengths. Respect is nice, but I had begun to hunger for love. Could anyone love me? Well, how could they? I let no one know me. I carefully hid all the parts of myself I considered unacceptable—my sexuality, my confusion, my self-doubt, my sadness, my loneliness. One evening I was walking with a "friend" (translate "comrade")—at least a guy who seemed interested in the parts of myself I had been willing to show. I suddenly got the crazy idea that maybe it was time to risk more of myself, and that this fellow might be the person with whom to do it. So I told him of my struggle and my need, and began opening up parts of my inner self I never shared with anyone. Suddenly I felt horribly exposed and embarrassed by what I had done. I was shaking, and my mouth was dry. My secret was out, and it might mean the end of all respect. Just when I was most vulnerable, he amazed me by responding to all I had said with the greatest gentleness, without any judgment. He was touched by what I had shared and began opening himself up to me as well. We walked, then sat, for another hour, talking about all this. When we parted, I found myself anxious again that he would have very different thoughts and probably distance himself, and that would be the end of the relationship. In fact, it proved to be the first real friendship of my life. We formed a strong bond. Forty years later we are still friends, and have more than once gone back gratefully to that day when we both broke through into a different way of being men.

In the years since, as a therapist and spiritual guide, I have listened to men tell me stories of some of the most important things that have ever happened to them. I have noticed that many seem to think that they are sharing feelings when they just narrate an event of great consequence. They might tell of childhood trauma, or of their divorce, or of the death of a child. The story itself is gripping. But as I listen, I find myself wondering, "Yes, but where are you in all this?" In other words, I hear the events, and I can *imagine* what you might be thinking and feeling, but you are not *telling* me any of that. Well, it is precisely that which I am most interested in, because it is that which lets me know you. You cannot just assume I will know it because you are telling the story. You have to tell me exactly what was going on inside you as it all unfolded. Your feelings are the crucial material. Isn't that what you really want me to understand, so that I catch the impact on you, and end by understanding you and your life better? Now go over it again, and let your feelings come, and let me see and hear them. Now I've got it. And now I am bonded with you.

So it is a recovery and reclamation project we are looking at here. Before any man is going to undertake this hard work, he has to see that he really needs to do it, that he is dwarfed as he stands. He has to be dissatisfied, and to have glimpsed far richer realms of life standing within his reach. He has to become convinced that it is better to be a real human being than the Marlboro Man. That realization, fully embraced, is the key to everything. It represents a change of heart, a death and the beginning of new life.

Reading Suggestions

In her *Intimate Strangers* (New York: HarperCollins, 1983), Lillian Rubin talks about marital disappointment and one of its key contributors, men's failure to share themselves. She tells of one survey in which husbands and wives were asked who their best friend was. Three quarters of the men named their wives. Two thirds of those wives named a friend outside the marriage, almost always a woman.

Eugene Gendlin sets forth his method of focusing clearly and helpfully in his little classic *Focusing* (New York: Bantam Books, 1981).

3

MASTERING ANGER AND VIOLENCE

There are two strong drives in us that we must master if we would be men. One is our aggression. The other is our sex drive. These are the topics of the next two chapters. It is possible that this whole chapter will turn you off, because it will seem extreme and about other men, not about you. Yet there is a violent streak even in the best of us, and it can become a very unruly feature of our lives. If you come out of this review still feeling that it has nothing to do with you, be glad and celebrate. Perhaps you could at least dedicate yourself more generously to eliminating this kind of behavior in the world, because it is a battle women probably cannot win without our help.

As I was mulling my approach to the issue of violence, there appeared in the Sunday newspaper three stories of male violence in various parts of the world—and none of the stories was about the many wars in which men are fighting. The first account was of domestic abuse in Vietnam. There, men exercise their responsibility for "teaching" their wives through beatings and other forms of abuse, in what researchers say is a virtual epidemic. Standing it, taking the blame for it, keeping quiet about it—this is how most Vietnamese women cope, even when they are the primary breadwinners in the family. Women simply have no recourse. There is an irony here. In Vietnam, official propaganda campaigns are regularly launched against "social evils" such as prostitution and drug abuse, but not a word is said about the rampant evil of violence against women in their homes. While reliable statistical data are hard to get, anecdotal evidence of acid attacks to the face and breasts, knifings, marital rape, burnings, and beatings abound. Husbands killing their wives accounted for about 14 percent of all killings in 1992; in 1997, it had risen to 20 percent.

A second story came out of Uzbekistan, an Asian country about the size of California. There, under one of the most authoritarian and brutal regimes of the fifteen countries that gained independence with the collapse of the U.S.S.R., some 5000 people have been imprisoned for their political or religious beliefs. Dozens have been executed, a dozen more tortured to death. A harsh new prison has been built in the remote desert in the closed city of Zhaslyk, which has become known as "the place from which no one returns." Many of those arrested have been tortured to get them to confess or implicate others. Methods include electric shocks, near suffocation, beatings with rubber sticks and plastic bottles filled with water. Relatives of arrested men say that one common form of torture is burning the penis.

We might wish to think that we are better than the men of other countries. I hope we are, but I am not so sure. A third story in that paper told of the large numbers of black slaves forced to build our nation's Capitol and White House, their "owners" being handsomely compensated for the slaves' services. What a blot on these two lasting monuments to American democracy and freedom. And anyone who knows the history of American slavery knows that the methods used to keep slaves in subjugation differed only in detail from the methods used in the two stories above. Our own military men use these same tactics in war. And our School of the Americas in Georgia, recently renamed because it is under such heavy criticism for what it is doing, was built to train personnel from the Latin American countries in precisely the same brutal tactics, in order to keep in place the governments the United States wants in place for the sake of our interests, whether those governments are corrupt or not.

Something closer to home may help us see that male violence is neither a narrowly confined problem nor a thing of the past. According to the F.B.I. Uniform Crime Report, 95,769 rapes were reported in the United States during 1996. That is one rape every six minutes. The incidence of rape is actually much higher, according to Linda Ledray from the Sexual Assault Resource Service in Minneapolis. She says that many victims do not report the crime because they fear the assailant, whose parting words in 76 percent of cases are: "If you tell anyone (or report anything to the police), I'll come back and kill you…rape you again…rape your child…." If legal and cultural structures in the United States did not wink at rape, there would probably be less of it. In reported rape incidents in the United States, over 50 percent of the perpetrators are arrested, yet only 4 percent end up in jail. The fact that rape is seldom punished not only provides a clear message to the rapist, but also to his victim.

If there is a thread running through these stories, it has to do with what many men believe it means to be a man. They might concede that the behavior got a little extreme in some of these cases, but they believe men need to be violent to win the constant competition against other men, and to make it perfectly clear to weaker men and, above all, to women who is boss. They love movies that glorify this kind of violence, especially when it crushes someone they do not like. They like football games, if their team is triumphant in the clash of forces. To them the world is such that it is either hit or be hit, kill or be killed. To be a man is to be tough (even feared), to be on top, and to wield coercive power over others. That is just the way it is. If this is the mindset you were raised in, it is difficult to change it. Yet many men who were conditioned this way have changed, adopting a different worldview and a different stance.

How Do We Change?

When some men hear of incidents like the above, their hearts go out to the victims. They feel compassion for them. They can imagine what it would be like to suffer that themselves. They can also imagine the effects of the violence on the victims' families and friends. Then they are struck by the basic unfairness of the situation. Men beating up women? Men torturing helpless victims to death? In other words, though they know the gratification of being top dog in relationships, they also know, or have heard others tell, what it feels like to be the underdog. That is compassion, and compassion is the key to conversion. That and a concern for fairness.

So if you are shocked when you hear accounts of the brutal ways that men torture other men physically, or how they gang-rape women to show them what trash they are; if you are pained when you hear accounts of men's sexual exploitation of children; if your sense of justice is offended when you read of gay men being beaten in the street by groups of straight men; if your heart goes out to women in situations of domestic violence from which they can find no escape; then you are a real man, that is, you are a human being. You are moving from being part of the problem to being part of the solution.

That is the crucial first step: an ethical decision born of compassion, that this is not right, and a wholehearted embracing of two consequences: I cannot behave this way myself, and I must join the struggle against this kind of injustice in the world.

A lot of male violence against women proceeds from a false sense of entitlement. If a woman rejects my overtures, I have the right to stalk her and make her life miserable. Who does she think she is to say no to me? If my wife opposes me, I have every right to vindicate myself by force. It simply belongs to being male. If she insults me, or calls my power (manhood) into question, I will avenge the offense and remind her who is boss. If my wife seeks divorce, and we have children, I might just have to kill her and the children, not only to hurt her, but so she will never forget that in the end all of them belong to me. This may sound appalling, but we see these beliefs being acted out. The underlying premise is male privilege, men's God-given right, and woe to anyone who fails to recognize it.

We can observe the same dynamic at work on a much larger scale in the wars between nations and ethnic groups. A wrong is done or at least perceived. The almost instinctive recourse is to violence to right that wrong. You hurt us, and we will hurt you back. We will show you what it feels like. In fact, we will hurt you more. Once the cycle of revenge begins, it can go on for hundreds of years. Countless lives are destroyed, and few can remember how it all got started.

Notice what is almost never done. Rarely is there any self-examination to discover what our side may have done wrong to provoke this anger and violence against us. Seldom is there any attempt to get together with people from the other side to learn what the problem is and how we might work together peaceably to solve it. There are two questions very few ask, and rarely are those who ask them in high places: "Is it morally right to do what we are contemplating?" "Is it strategically effective in the long run, or will it just keep the violence going?" A brief statement of Martin Luther King, Jr., which appeared on cards distributed after the September 11, 2001, terrorist attacks on the United States, speaks eloquently to these questions:

Darkness cannot drive out darkness;
Only light can do that.
Hate cannot drive out hate;
Only love can do that.

Hate multiplies hate,
Violence multiplies violence,
And toughness multiplies toughness
In a descending spiral of destruction...
The chain reaction of evil—
Hate begetting hate,
Wars producing more wars—
Must be broken,
Or we shall be plunged into
The darkness of annihilation.

Well aware of the level technology had reached, he proclaimed in another place that we have just two alternatives: "It is either non-violence, or non-existence." What a challenge. What an immense moral conversion is called for here. But is he wrong?

Anger and Violence

Much violence is quite coolly enacted, no particular anger being present, just a conviction that this is what a man has to do. But anger is sometimes the culprit in violence. Anger rises in a man, and he lashes out violently. Many a man's wife is afraid of him; so are his children. He has displayed that fierce and wild streak on occasion, and in their gut they fear for their safety—even if he has not yet ever hit or throttled them. Some men will say, "That is the way they ought to feel." Others will say, "I feel ashamed that I have put them in that kind of fear. What kind of beast have I been? It is simply not fair for me to prevail in the family by using physical force."

A client of mine told of doing some work at the home of his aging father. On top of a cabinet in the kitchen, he came upon a switch his father had used to keep him and his brothers in line. It set off a powerful visceral reaction in him, almost knocking him off his chair. He perspired and grew faint before he could step down and recover. As he recounted this to me, he recalled telling his dad as an adult how he and his brothers had feared that he might kill them. They had watched him kill many an animal on their farm. "That is the way I wanted it," his father said. "That is what boys need to keep them from doing what they shouldn't do."

But do boys or girls or women or men need this sort of deterrent to help them choose the good? I hold out a lot more hope for dialogue, and, in the case of children, consequences of a far less cruel nature. I do know that as men we need some guidelines for the management of our anger. I would suggest four.

1. *It is OK to be angry, to say that you are angry, and to say why; it is not OK to vent anger.* To vent anger is to be physically violent with the person you are angry at, to throw things, slam doors, pound on tables, put your fist through the wall, or abuse verbally. These are actions that establish a reign of terror and do serious damage to relationships. Men's anger-management groups insist on a foundational principle:

> We choose to be abusive; we can choose not to be.
> We learn to be abusive; we can learn not to be.

Men's anger management groups are probably the best way to go if you have trouble controlling your anger.

2. *If you are too hot to maintain good control of your behavior, leave the scene.* Excuse yourself, and go someplace where you can sit and deep-breathe yourself back down to calmness. You can walk it off or burn it off by doing some physical work. During this time you can also reflect on what has happened, what the other person seems to be trying to say and how you want to respond to that, what is at stake for you here, what you want to say and how you want to say it. Now, since you broke off the conversation by leaving, it is your responsibility to

reopen it—but now calmly, and with a clearer sense of how to proceed constructively. This is how both of you learn something, both of you get something out of the conflict, both of you grow. The other path is mere destruction.

3. *When someone else is expressing anger at you, listen awhile before you speak.* This person is passionately trying to get something across to you. What they most need is the feeling that you respect them enough to take it in and think about it. If you defend yourself or fight them, you fan the flames of their frustration. If you listen and respond by letting them know that you got their point(s) and even agree to some extent, they will probably calm down. Then you can state your side of the matter.

4. *Do something about the remote causes of your anger.* If you find yourself getting angry a lot even over relatively trivial matters, there is probably a deeper unhappiness that has you at a high threshold of irritability. Maybe it is your work or the general direction of your life. Maybe it is fatigue or multiple stresses at this time. Perhaps it is larger issues in the relationship with the person you are angry with now over some small thing. Perhaps it is experiences from your childhood or from a previous relationship that you have never adequately processed. The key to getting at a state of high irritability is to dig deeper and deal with the underlying issues. A psychologist who works with battered women and battering men thinks wife-battering is often a substitute for tears. A man dare not speak of his fear or hurt, or even allow them to exist, so he expresses them as violence against the one who somehow brings them to awareness. Violence can also be a compensation for inner deadness, to make a man feel alive again when he is frozen emotionally.

Sometimes the underlying issue in an angry man is depression, a chronic state of feeling emotionally down. When depression is acute, it is easy to recognize; it cuts sharply into one's ability to function. But when it lies in a lower register, and has been around for years, it might escape notice for the illness it is, and just be accepted as part of life. The sufferer thinks that his state is how it is for everyone. It is not.

Men often hesitate to ask for help, but this chronic state of low-level depression I speak of does not represent any kind of personal failure or weakness. It is physiological in origin, often hereditary, and does not answer to an act of the will. It is like diabetes, a physiological condition, though the illness of depression also affects the emotions. It can usually be alleviated with medication. Fortunately, in our day many medications are available. If you usually feel down and are prone to silence and brooding; if you have to struggle to get out of bed and face your day; if life seems mostly hard and genuine pleasure is a rare event; if you have difficulty concentrating or making decisions; if you tend to withdraw from people into your own lonely space; if you are inclined to drink to feel better; if you find embers of anger deep down and high irritability accompanying your heaviness of heart, you are suffering from the condition I describe. Get a psychiatric evaluation, not because you are crazy but because you have a mental illness that is interfering with your best possibilities, and accept medication if it is suggested. I have seen it make a huge difference in many people's lives. Once you have a clearer head, a better mood, and more energy, you will be able to address whatever other issues you may need to work on with a therapist.

Violence is a huge issue for men, the havoc it wreaks in the world visible on every side. So is anger. They are not the same, but they are often related. We need to make an ethical commitment not to use violence to deal with differences, or to establish or maintain our maleness and mastery. We also need to learn how to control the energy of our anger and direct it toward constructive rather than destructive ends.

Reading Suggestions

The opening three stories all appeared in the first section of the *Seattle Times*, Sunday, July 23, 2000.

Terrence Real, *I Don't Want to Talk about It: Overcoming the Secret Legacy of Male Depression* (New York: Simon & Schuster, 1997), offers a thorough analysis of what he calls "covert male depression" and its healing through medication and therapy.

For a description of how gangs work, and how to deal with young people involved in them, see Curtis W. Branch, ed., *Adolescent Gangs: Old Issues, New Approaches* (Hove, UK/New York: Brunner-Routledge, 1999).

Kathleen Fischer, *Transforming Fire: Women Using Anger Creatively* (Mahwah, NJ: Paulist Press, 1999), though addressed mainly to women, offers a matchless analysis of anger's roots, varied expressions, and constructive management.

4

PUTTING SEX AND LOVE TOGETHER

Our sexuality is the second strong drive we have to master if we would be men. And it is indeed a strong drive. It is emptiness and yearning. It is curiosity, attraction, appetite. We are aware of it often, particularly in the presence of sexual opportunity—or in its too-long absence.

Because the male sex drive is so powerful, it jumps the tracks sometimes. A boy might expose himself to younger children, cajole them into showing him their private parts, even force sexual activity on a younger sibling or neighbor. A teenager or young adult male can allow sex to become so consuming that he is largely taken up with one objective: sexual gratification. So can a middle-aged man, or even an older man. And his prey may not even be adults. These manifestations of male sexuality, so damaging to others, tell us something that we need to know: We are dealing with a very powerful force here, one that can do great harm. It needs to be tamed.

Perhaps that is the reason why a sense of shame so often attends sexuality. We do not easily talk about it, even with other men. We would be embarrassed to admit how large a factor it is in our lives, how pervasive our preoccupation with it, how destructively we have sometimes surrendered to the power of sex. We recognize how easily sex can get out of proportion in the whole scheme of things.

God is a great gambler. God gives every boy a penis. With that wonderful gift comes a profoundly challenging responsibility: to humanize the force and integrate it into genuine loving. Sexuality is in this respect like many other parts of our predicament. We are not born human beings. We are born with the ingredients of human being, and it is up to us to fashion them into something that can truly be called human. We are given a mound of clay, and ours is the task of making it into something that looks like a person.

What Is a Woman?

We do not choose our sexual orientation. We find ourselves with it. It manifests itself as an attraction to certain persons, more commonly persons of the opposite sex, sometimes persons of the same sex. Here I go with the predominant case, a man's attraction to women, and talk about what it means to humanize it and integrate sexuality into genuine loving. But all the same principles apply to same-sex attraction.

When a man sees a woman who is attractive to him, he "turns on." He is stirred. She seizes his attention. His gaze follows her, studies her, muses on her. His heart warms. He may even feel a genital stirring. He is under a bit of a spell, slightly hypnotized. He is curious, definitely drawn. He wants what she has, what she is. The whole experience has more than a touch of magic in it, so it is sometimes called "chemistry." His reaction to her is so fascinating and productive of movement in him that it has inspired a vast outpouring of music and poetry, not to mention reams of philosophy, psychology, and theology.

Up to this point, the man has no choice. All of this just happens to him, as by some program in nature. It occurs every time the right kind of woman comes into his personal space. It just stirs, that's all, awakening a set of feelings strange and wonderful. But now he has a choice. What is he going to do with this? For that he is responsible.

A man has to talk to himself. He has to think and take charge. He has to convert raw instinct into a genuinely human response. Yes, she is beautiful and attractive. Yes, she is vulnerable. But she is not an object. She is a subject. She is not a thing, and she does not exist for me. She is a subject, and she exists for herself, as my sister does, and my mother, and myself. She has a life, goals, feelings, friends, projects. I have to respect her freedom and her boundaries. And she has an agenda right now as she walks by, her own, which most likely has nothing whatsoever to do with me. She is her own person, and she is my equal, no more at my disposal than I am at hers. She does not exist for my gratification, except as an object of contemplation, like the rest of nature. All of this puts matters into another perspective entirely. It puts a bridle on my horse. I have remembered that she is a human being, and, in realizing that, have come back to my own humanity.

I can still enjoy her beauty and praise whatever made her and sent her my way. I can even talk to her, if opportunity offers—but always I will respect her freedom. And if I appreciate what she is, just in herself, I will make myself part of her protection network so that no one else violates her either.

By this inner process, which I have to go through again and again until it becomes habit, I have humanized my sexuality and integrated it into responsible loving. It is still alive and active in me, still a dimension of my delight in and motion toward an attractive woman, still a powerful force. But it is no longer a raw force, reckless and lethal. It has been embraced into a larger whole, my personhood. I will have to continue doing this work of integration all my life, toward all women and girls, even toward my wife. For marriage is not the acquisition of a piece of property either. My wife is ever a subject, equal in dignity and right, with a life all her own. What she gives to me is always a free gift. When her needs coalesce with my needs, her wants with my wants, it is serendipity. When they do not, it cannot be helped. She is not my possession but my partner. I disappoint her too.

What Is This Insatiable Hunger?

There is another whole side to our inner reflection and eventual discoveries about our sex drive. If we are willing to spend some time mentally inside it, and reflect on the sexual and other relational experiences we have had, we will begin to understand what this imperious need is at root, or what it is for which we really yearn.

If we have never dreamed that a woman might be a person, and would not want to hear it if someone tried to tell us, if we have gone for the gusto and been successful at laying a number of women, we know that our "conquests" have brought us no real satisfaction. We may continue to do it, because we cannot think of anything better to do, or because the compulsion, or addiction, remains strong. But we know that the empty place inside is not filled up by this sort of thing. We have seen, more than once, a woman deeply pained. And we have despised ourselves. There is a promising side to our inner conflict. Our potential humanity is trying to get our attention.

If we are willing to take stock of this, and spend more time mentally inside our sex drive, what might we learn? That our sex drive and our loneliness, another familiar companion, are one, and that both are pushing us toward what we are made for: relationship and generativity.

We are made for relationship. We are essentially social. We *need* other people, not just for survival, but in order to develop and become ourselves. And then we still yearn for someone to really love, who will really love us back. What we long for is intimacy, real closeness with at least one person. That is what the sexual hunt is really all about. Sex is just a symbol of the intimacy we crave with another human being. The real thing is knowing and being known, loving and being loved—emotional, spiritual union, with mutual affirmation and support. Often the best experiences of this have no sexual component at all.

If someday we receive that great gift of the coming togeth... of human hearts in love, and remain still attentive to what goes on inside us, we will discover another surprise. We are still not satisfied! In fact, even if we manage to add the good job, the great house, and the plump bank account to our intimate relationship, we are still not satisfied. The whole world is not enough. St. Augustine spoke to our situation fifteen centuries ago, and we can still recognize the truth of his words: "You have made us for yourself, O God, and our hearts are restless until they rest in you." This is another piece of the puzzle of our loneliness. Our heart's capacity is larger than anything and everything that is available to us in this dimension. Its ache points toward a transcendent destiny.

The other need buried in our loneliness (and sex drive) is our longing to be generative. Generativity is the giving of life. Again, sex is just the symbol. Many a sex act generates a new life, but that is not what was sought nor is it even valued. Yet we do deeply desire to give life—to something, to someone. We need to love, to give ourselves, to bring something into being that is good. We need to live for more than ourselves, to be part of some larger movement or project. We want to give something to the world. We want our lives to make a difference. That is what generativity is, and getting into it in some form is essential to our happiness. Most generativity is not sexual at all. The teacher is generative, the artist, the coach. Their lives make a difference, and in that they find meaning and satisfaction, even though it exacts a price. This desire to give life runs deep in us, telling us something more of what we are made for.

So we may or may not find a sexual partner. We may or may not ever generate a child. But we can and must enjoy intimacy, and we can and must be generative if we want to be fulfilled as human beings. Our sex drive and our loneliness are there to keep propelling us toward these things. And we need the push, because intimacy and generativity are both difficult. In both, we have to give, and risk, and suffer, to receive the rewards they bring. Both of these needs are deeper and broader than mere sexual activity. We will be intimate, hopefully, with many more people than we will ever have sex with, and generative in the lives of many more people too, in a rich variety of ways.

If the above analysis is correct, maybe it is not sex itself that we need or want so badly, even when the drive is strongest. Our sex drive may be just a manifestation of deeper personal needs.

What Is Love?

Let us come back to that woman who passed by. What would it mean to love her instead of just wanting her? It all revolves around her well-being. To love her would be to care about her well-being and happiness, and to put ourselves out to further them. It would be self-transcending. It would be for her. If we got good things out of our care for her well-being, all the better, and we probably would. But that is strictly secondary in love. It is not in the driver's seat; it is just a passenger. Love is most itself when it asks nothing at all of what has captured its devotion. It just rejoices in it and lets it be itself. It only wants to protect it, nurture it, and help it get where it is trying to go.

A woman is a sexual being too, but in a different way. She is not so driven to the physical gratification of sex. Nor is she a hunter in the same way. Her sexual fantasies run not so much to fantastic sex as to fantastic love—to be wanted, to be cherished, to be protected, to settle down and create a family with someone. She also wants to give the gift of herself and watch her love bring good things into being. She is typically much more in touch with her desire for intimacy and generativity in the broad sense than a man is. She does not face the same task of sexual integration a man faces. Empty sex holds little allure for her, though she might engage in it to please a man, in the hopes of forming a deeper bond with him.

If a man is handsome, she notices and enjoys it. But that quality is not very high on her list of priorities. Where it exists, she hopes it symbolizes the fact that he is a gentleman, beautiful on the inside too. What she seeks is a mate who is genuinely interested in her as a person, not just as a beautiful body. And a man who is himself interesting as a person, a man with something inside. For how could she be intimate with a man who is empty? What is there to relate to? His penis? His muscles?

Just recently a man came for counseling whose only problem, he said, was that there was no woman in his life. He just couldn't find one, or attract one, or something. As I got to know him better, I began to see what the problem was. This is what I told him. Your best chance of meeting a good woman lies in doing some work on yourself. You are unhappy. There is no woman in the world who can make you happy, and only a foolish woman would take you on as a project. Each of us has to make our own happiness, and then we will begin to be attractive as a person, male or female. An attractive man is one who is happy. He already has a life. He is at peace with himself, his work, other people. He already has friends, because he loves. He gives himself, broadly and generously, to the world. Two other qualities are conspicuous in his presentation. He has the capacity to enjoy the little things, the best things in life, which are free. And he has a sense of humor. That man is attractive. He does not have to hunt very hard. He will be found. He is exactly what *she* is looking for.

Two Norms for Sexual Relating

Exploitive or empty sex is neither satisfying nor worthy of ethical approval. People in our culture tend to rush into sex before the foundations for good sex are laid in a relationship, and often enough come away from their encounters hurt or at least dissatisfied. A man who wants to be a good person knows that there are ethical considerations in his sexual relating, and he seeks guidelines for his behavior. What might those guidelines be?

Most of us in this culture were raised as Christians and were given some sort of sexual instruction in that connection. Taking another look at the sexual teaching of Jesus seems a good place to start our search for norms, partly because a lot of subsequent church teaching has been broadly ascribed to him though it was not his, and partly because he does have some genuinely helpful things to say.

A close examination of the gospels turns up very little in the way of a sexual ethic. Jesus says nothing at all, for instance, about masturbation, premarital sex, or homosexuality. Nor does he extol celibacy, as if the whole topic of sexuality were unworthy of consideration by a spiritual person. It is at a wedding, in fact, that Jesus chooses to perform one of his most lavish signs, the changing of a large quantity of water into wine to enhance the celebration. He does take a clear position against adultery and for marital permanence. And he speaks against a man's lusting after a woman in his heart (this just a single line, and, interestingly, appearing in only one of the four gospels, Matt 5:28). Here he calls us men on our tendency to see women as mere sexual objects, encouraging us to reverence them as persons with their own dignity and their own lives.

While he offers little sexual instruction, Jesus does speak to the issue in exhibiting an immense concern for the quality of human relationships. It is here that he gives us the norm we seek. It is a moral/spiritual ideal. His single, overarching principle for all of our relating is genuine human love. Our question, then, is: What implications does this norm have for sexual relating?

One way to see a matter clearly is to start from the opposite side. It is clear that sex can hurt people, and hurting people is not a good way to love them. Sex hurts people when it is violent or abusive, when it seeks self-gratification without regard for the feelings or well-being of the other person. The two worst cases of it are taking sexual advantage of a child for one's own gratification, and rape. Both are traumatic events for the victim, profoundly damaging, very hard to heal. But sexual exploitation has other forms too: the man ever on the sexual hunt who leads women on, the man who sexually harasses women, the man who acts considerately toward his mate only when he wants sex from her, the man so bent on his own pleasure that he has little regard for his partner's pleasure or pain. These are abusive actions, disrespectful of the dignity of the other person, clearly unloving.

Two more specific norms suggest themselves for breaking Jesus' love commandment down for clearer application to sexual relating: *authenticity* and *responsibility*. *Authenticity* means being honest, a challenging ideal in sexual relating where it is so easy to pretend in order to get what one wants. *Responsibility* means being careful, soberly assessing consequences and being genuinely concerned for the welfare of one's mate, oneself, and any life that may result from sexual relating. Being honest and being careful rule out sexuality's most common abuses: exploitation, promiscuity, careless pregnancy, and the transmission of disease. All of these obviously hurt other people, and ourselves as well, and hence violate the love commandment.

Those who would love truly need to keep their communication open as they keep testing their developing sexual relationship for authenticity and responsibility. It is not uncommon in a developing relationship for sex to start early and soon lead the way, so that when the couple is together, they are sharing physical intimacies much more than really getting to know one another or facing issues they need to talk about. This is inauthentic, because all the physical tenderness being expressed is way ahead of the actual bond between them. Let an unexpected pregnancy occur and the two quickly realize how completely unprepared they are to make a life together in support of this child. Even short of pregnancy, if we listen closely to our own hearts, and hear our mate out in dialogue, we will often enough find that one or other of us is not entirely comfortable with the way our sexual intimacy fits into the larger picture of our relationship and our lives.

Our sexuality is a great and wonderful gift. It stirs joy, gratitude, and awe in us. It also has a moral dimension. It lives in us as a powerful relational force that needs to be harnessed, humanized, and integrated. Learning to integrate our sexuality into genuine loving is quite a task. But it must be accomplished if we would be men.

Reading Suggestions

For a fine development of the idea of sexuality as lively dynamism toward relatedness, see Judith Plaskow, *Standing Again at Sinai: Judaism from a Feminist Perspective* (New York: HarperCollins, 1991).

Some books by Christian pastors and theologians who regard sexuality positively and take an intelligently nuanced approach to its moral norms are Evelyn Eaton Whitehead and James D. Whitehead, *Wisdom of the Body: Making Sense of Our Sexuality* (New York: Crossroad, 2001); James B. Nelson, *Embodiment: An Approach to Sexuality and Christian Theology* (Minneapolis: Augsburg, 1978), and *Between Two Gardens: Reflections on Sexuality and Religious Experience* (Cleveland: Pilgrim Press, 1983). Thomas Fox, in his *Sexuality and Catholicism* (New York: George Braziller, 1995), gives us the history of Roman Catholic thought on sexual issues from ancient times to the present.

James B. Nelson and Sandra Longfellow, eds., *Sexuality and the Sacred* (Louisville, KY: Westminster John Knox, 1994), is a collection of essays exploring the presence of the Mystery in human sexuality.

5

LOOKING FOR A MATE

The main focus of this chapter is the search for a person with whom to share your life. In the life of most men, straight or gay, that becomes a priority sooner or later, as the desire grows to settle down and make a life with someone. But it is not always so easy to find that person. There are, besides, considerations that hold many a man back, like the freedom he will lose, and the scary bringing of closure to what had always been an open-ended situation. We will consider the many issues concerned with the search for that special someone, then reflect briefly on a related search—for good men friends. Some of the issues overlap.

Bob was in his forties. Although he had never been married, he had enjoyed many relationships with women over the past twenty years. For most of that time he had not been terribly interested in marrying, but that was changing. He felt ready to settle down, and was now sizing up his partners more and more in terms of lifelong companionship. But no one was emerging. He would go with someone for a while, and the relationship would be promising, but something important would always be missing. She might be educated and interested in the spiritual life, both important to Bob, but there would be no chemistry. Or the sex would be great, but she would not be someone Bob could look forward to a life with as a personal equal. Or she might be smart and spiritual and attractive, but be too serious. "Is there something wrong with *me*?" Bob began to wonder. "Am I looking for perfection? Am

I afraid of intimacy or commitment, so that I keep looking for some reason to say no?"

He was asking good questions, and we sifted and sorted through his many relationship experiences and his personal history. Fear of intimacy and of commitment are real obstacles for quite a few people, and often there are unresolved childhood issues in the mix as well. In Bob's case, those did not seem to be the problem, nor was he insisting that his mate be perfect, another sure stopper. The main problem was rather that at midlife, with all his education, experience, and the work he had done on his personal growth, he could hardly make a life with someone who was not, generally speaking, his equal. And that woman had not yet appeared. I know many men and women in this predicament, highly realized individuals with whom it would be a joy to live. But finding someone enough like themselves for a partnership that will play out well over time is very difficult.

Where and How to Look

Where can I find the person of my dreams?

My first suggestion is, go where people are doing what you love to do. Those gathered there are like you in at least one significant respect. Go dancing if you love to dance. Join a book club if you love to read. Don't go to the bars unless you are looking for an alcoholic or a one-night stand. Go hiking if you love the outdoors. Do political or other volunteering if that is what you love. Meeting people in a group-setting like this where there is shared activity, where neither of you is on trial as on a blind date, but where you can do some observing and strike up conversations as you feel drawn, is a much more natural, less stressful, way to spot and meet a person of interest.

For that matter, wherever it is you already gather with others—school, church, work—look around you, because there is opportunity here too. Cultivate acqaintanceship and friendship. One may grow into something quite special. A solid friendship is, after all, the core of a good marriage. And what is a friendship? A relationship rooted in common interests, common values, and the genuine enjoyment of each other. These are the things that last.

What about the Internet, the personals, or matching services as ways to find her? There is nothing wrong with any of these avenues, and some people have found what they sought by one of them. There is usually quite a bit of sorting through to be done, and sometimes none of those who present themselves are quite right. But that is the way it usually is in the search for a mate, no matter what approach you take. It is a low-odds proposition. It can be very discouraging. You have to realize that going in and accept it again and again if you are going to persevere. Why is it low-odds? Because each of us is a complex universe, and it is not easy to find someone that we would want to live with—who also wants to live with us. That is asking a lot. Not that there are not plenty of good people around, but this is a very special assignment.

Let your friends know that you are looking for a mate. Ask them to introduce you to anyone that they think might be a candidate. It will bring people your way whom you would not otherwise find, and who come with a recommendation from someone who knows you well.

This all sounds very practical, but the thought of actually getting into the search brings many a man up against one of the main enemies of much human action—fear. What are some of your fears, and how can you deal with them?

The Fears

A man's first fear often is: Would any woman want me—I mean, a woman I would want? Should I even present myself? Should I get a hairstylist? A body trainer? A dress coach? I need them all! And they would not even touch my deeper problems.

I am not rich. I am not a good conversationalist. And when it comes to sex, I am not any too sure of myself.

As uncomfortable as these feelings of self-doubt and vulnerability are, they are actually endearing, so human are they. And humility is a much more attractive quality than pride every time. Your parents felt these feelings before you. Your children will feel them after you. The woman you will meet is feeling them too, wondering if you could possibly be interested in her. Which of us can be much other than we are? But somehow we are lovable this way, at least to some people.

While there is value in looking your best, that is not mainly what the matter turns on. It turns on who you are, and on whether that appeals to a particular person. Who you are is the product of your entire history to this point, and has many dimensions. How much you might appeal to a given person is entirely out of your control. There is only one thing you can do: Be yourself, and see what happens. What you are is hard to change all that much, and hard to hide for very long, so there is little use pretending. The good news is, it is enough. Look around you at the people who are married. Are they all svelte, brilliant, handsome, charming, rich? By no means. Yet they somehow got mates. Not only sexually, but in every other way, both of you bring doubts and wounds and limited experience, and will be helping and teaching each other. The relationship grows precisely by your working through together all the challenges that you meet.

Fear of intimacy is another great stopper. Intimacy means being close, and that is scary. Being close means being known. When you get to know me, you might reject me. That would really hurt. Also, if we become intimate, you can make demands on me. In some way, we will belong to one another. That scares me too. You might take me over. There might be too much of you and too little of me. I'm not sure that I'm strong enough to hold my ground and remain myself in a close relationship. And then another thought comes. If we get close and share life as a couple, I will come to need you. What if you leave me? What if you die? I have loved and lost before, and it was horrible. I vowed that I would never let it happen again. All things considered, intimacy is terrifying, and I think I better let it go.

That is before we even talk about commitment, which may be the most frightening part of all. Saying yes to you means saying no to every other woman. That is a death I'm not sure I want to die. Saying yes to you also means I'm trapped—for life. I see a heavy metal door descending over my freedom. Today, I can come and go as I please. And all my options are still open. When a woman starts making demands on me, I just remind her that I am under no obligation. If she doesn't like the terms, she can pack up and go. Commitment! What if it doesn't work? What a mess. Public embarrassment. Killer emotions. Kids left in the lurch. I have seen it, and I want no part of it. Better to avoid all entanglements. Hang loose. Who knows, maybe someday the perfect woman will just walk into my life, and I will know. Yes, I think I will wait.

No question about it, the hazards are real. This is serious business. Intimacy is risky. Commitment does close doors. And it sometimes all falters and fails, leaving a man crushed and desolate. Some have sought for years without finding, and it is not because of some defect in their makeup. Many have entered relationships and really bonded, then run into problems that they could not work through, and come away bereft and in deep grief. We need to give ourselves time to heal when this happens, seeking God's support and that of good friends. And then it takes a lot of courage to reach out and try again.

If it is this risky, why does anyone seek and then enter into an intimate, committed relationship? Because they believe the benefits outweigh the risks, and they are willing to incur the dangers to reap the rewards. Intimacy is something our hearts crave, and, found, it is wonderful. Sexuality is a great gift that we long to enjoy. So are children. Commitment is an incomparable treasure. It means that we can bank on one another through thick and thin, all the way into the darkness of death. Besides, even with the struggles, and largely because of them, committed relationships make human beings out of us. Marriage is a great school of love, from which we never graduate. At death's door, we are still trying to get it right—the daunting challenge of loving even one human being well. In the process we are slowly transformed, as we learn humility, acceptance, patience, fairness, and loyalty.

In the end, there are, it seems, two basic approaches to life. One is to wade in, engage it, grapple with what comes, learn and grow from all the experience. The other is to stay on the shore, hire scouts, arrange to watch it on television. The latter course has its enthusiasts, for the sake of its one clear reward—safety. But which course offers more satisfaction? The former, most of us would agree, even with the toil and suffering that it entails. C. S. Lewis has some remarks on the specific hazards of love.

> To love at all is to be vulnerable. Love anything, and your heart will certainly be wrung and possibly be broken. If you want to make sure of keeping it intact, you must give your heart to no one, not even to an animal. Wrap it carefully round with hobbies and little luxuries; avoid all entanglements; lock it up safe in the casket or coffin of your selfishness. But in that casket—safe, dark, motionless, airless—it will change. It will not be broken; it will become unbreakable, impenetrable, irredeemable. The alternative to tragedy, or at least to the risk of tragedy, is damnation. The only place outside heaven where you can be perfectly safe from all the dangers and perturbations of love is hell.

Some Common Mistakes

How can you enhance your chances of success in bonding deeply and staying bonded with someone? Let us look at some of the mistakes people commonly make that hurt their chances.

One mistake is to send off-putting signals. I have known many people who long to meet a mate, but you would never know it from the way they present themselves in public. They do not reach out. They do not smile. They do not even make eye contact. When we see people who carry themselves this way, we usually presume that they wish to be left alone. Who would guess that what they really want is human contact? If that is what we want, we have to present ourselves as open and inviting. I will always remember a brief Dear Abby letter and its response. "Dear Abby, I am 30, attractive, and would like to meet a man. Should I wear a badge that says, 'I'm available?'" "No need for the badge," Abby replies. "Just make eye contact and smile."

Another common mistake is to pretend to be something you are not, to make what you deem to be the desired impression. What sense does that make? You are looking for a life partner, which means you have to know how compatible the real he or she is with the real you. Don't pretend to be an extravert if you are really an introvert. Don't feign a sudden love for camping if you do not really enjoy it. Don't show enthusiasm for children if actually you do not want children. Don't pretend that you are a big spender if you are actually a saver. Marriage is long. How long can you pretend? Isn't it fairer, and wiser, to declare yourself up front, and give your partner a free choice based on the facts?

I recall a man who was so ashamed of his herpes that he said nothing about it until he and the woman he had come to love were on the very brink of their first sexual encounter. They had known each other several months, were very open with each other about many personal things, and had built a deep trust and closeness. Now this. What bothered the woman was not so much his herpes as that he had withheld this important information from her through all this time. What else might he be hiding?

There is another very common mistake that I call "floor-boarding it." It is the opposite of taking your time and respecting the organic processes of nature, which work slowly and imperceptibly. If you enter a relationship that seems to have promise, don't set your whole life aside and devote all your time and energy to this one thing. Go to work, keep up your home, get your rest, enjoy your other friends and activities. There is no need to call each other every day, let alone get together daily or spend every weekend together. No need to dive into the sack. If there is something of substance in the relationship, it will grow even when you are not tending it. If there is not, your efforts to push it where you want it to go will come to nothing. It takes two, and it takes time. It grows the way your hair does, or the seeds you planted in the ground. You cannot push nature. Greek novelist Nikos Kazantzakis tells a childhood story of the day he saw a butterfly struggling to come out of its cocoon. It did not seem to be making it, so he took the cocoon in his hands and pulled its fibers open further. That seemed to help. Then he noticed that the butterfly was all wet, and he blew on it to dry it for flight. Apparently encouraged, the butterfly struggled harder. Then it died.

A final mistake is more one of belief than of tactics. It is to approach the quest as if the mate you seek is going to be your salvation. You might believe that your life is on hold, perhaps not even started, until you find her. You think that everyone who is mated is happy, while you are miserable. You believe that the partnered have social respectability, while you have none. They have great sex lives and plenty of money, while you have neither. If they have children, they are even more blissful and fulfilled. Well, if this is what you think, you have not talked with any of these people lately. Talk to them. Yes, there are great goods in committed relationships. But the lives of the married are filled with problems and challenges too, so bad sometimes that they wish they were single again! To marry is not to say goodbye to all your woes and live happily ever after. It is to exchange one set of challenges for another—while a good many of the old ones hang around too. Some people *choose* not to marry. Some know that they are not the marrying kind. Others want different things from life more than they want marriage.

If it is someone who will "save you" and make you happy you are seeking, you have set yourself up for failure. Life is hard, and no one can save us from its pain. No one can make us happy either. Each of us is responsible for our own happiness, and it must always be made from the ingredients at hand, whatever our circumstances. Happiness is much more a matter of inner attitude than of outer circumstance, as many a human example bears witness. And the really attractive person is someone who is already happy, as we have seen.

So one of the best preparations for marriage is to learn to be a happy unmarried person, and to live this phase of your life as if it might be your last. But what makes for happiness, over and above a positive attitude? British essayist Joseph Addison once described the ingredients this way. Happiness is: something to do, something to love, something to hope for. That is a power-packed triad. Happiness is engagement with life. It is satisfying work, satisfying relationships, satisfying leisure activities, a few hopes not yet realized but striven for, and, I would add, at the heart of it all a strong relationship with the Mystery.

If these things are in place, then when you find a mate, your expectations will be much more likely to be realized. You will be looking not for your salvation, but only for someone to do the great adventure of life with, someone to help and be helped by, and someone to wrestle with as you learn how to love.

Men Friends

Men all too rarely have real friends in other men. It is a sad lack. There is something wonderful in solid friendship between two men, something qualitatively different from that close friendship which a good marriage also is. I know this experience well from the twenty-one years I lived as a Jesuit. We had freely set aside the satisfactions of intimacy with a woman and all that marriage and family life have to offer for the sake of total dedication to the service of God and our fellow human beings. We lived in all-male communities. And there grew up among us some remarkable friendships. I don't mean the entire community's solidarity, but men in two's, individuals with an affinity for one another developing a friendship and living from its energy. This had nothing to do with sex. Its heart and soul was emotional and spiritual sharing, a warm caring for one another born of appreciation, and abundant mutual support. In each of the various communities I lived in over the years, I was fortunate enough to enjoy this kind of friendship with one or two other men, and it went a long way toward sustaining me. I remember those friendships with the keenest appreciation. Some of them have survived my departure from the Jesuits. I see far too little of this in our culture, and it seems a tragic absence. I know it is possible, but to find it men have to approach one another in a different way than we have usually learned to do.

Our usual approach is competitive. We size each other up for strengths and weaknesses and compete for dominance, as male animals do to determine who will lead the pack and win access to the females. What we end up with, if we do not make enemies of each other, is camaraderie around shared activities, a value as far as it goes, but a clear second-best to intimacy and friendship. It all started when we were boys. Though even as boys we yearned for emotional connection, we enjoyed very little of it with each other. We spent most of our time with our male "friends" playing competitive games, teasing one another, and pretending to be grown men as we understood that concept. Many of us got so little grounding in emotional communication that we hardly know what intimacy is. In fact, in the culture of cruelty we inhabited with other boys, we might well have lost all trust. That is what makes male friendship so difficult now.

To find that great treasure today, we have to go against our conditioning. We have to make ourselves vulnerable. We have to be humbler and truer, opening up the softer inner core. Not with everyone, by any means. And not all at once. Choosing a man with whom we feel more affinity and a greater degree of safety than we do with most, we share, bit by bit, like trial balloons, parts of our inner selves that allow him to know us more fully. I mean more of our feelings, our pain and struggle, our desires, our hopes, our fears. If we meet with misunderstanding or a lack of reverence, we stop. Not too much has been lost. If we find that supportive hearing we hoped for, we give out even more. Another form of encouragement is when the other man feels invited by our personal sharing to share in kind, and he begins to do so. This is how genuine friendship begins to develop.

In this description, which is also an invitation, you will recognize strains of earlier music—how women bond with one another, what women want from their mates, and how men need to recover their lost life of feeling and begin to share more of it as part of their journey to healing and wholeness.

Some men hold back from getting close to other men for fear it will end in homosexuality. Unfamiliar with the territory, they fear that if men open up to one another, they are either showing they are gay whether they admit it or not, or will soon be into sexual expression. This is a false fear. It simply does not happen—unless both men really are gay. Straight men can enjoy deep friendship with each other without feeling drawn toward sexual expression.

Getting there is a matter of setting false fears aside, choosing those individuals whom we would like to have as friends, and opening ourselves more. When that deeper connection results, it is a gift to be cherished.

Reading Suggestions

Barry Neil Kaufman, *Happiness Is a Choice* (New York: Ballantine Books, 1991), deals ably with the thesis in his title. So does Anthony de Mello, more from an eastern wisdom perspective, in his *Awareness* (New York: Doubleday, 1990), a book invaluable as well for the rest of its keen insights.

James B. Nelson, *The Intimate Connection* (Philadelphia: Westminster, 1988), details the path to male friendship by making oneself vulnerable, and also with the obstacle to male friendship posed by homophobia.

Deborah Tannen, *You Just Don't Understand: Women and Men in Conversation* (New York: HarperCollins, 1990), deals with the different approaches men and women typically take to conversation. Her research shows that a man engages the world as an individual in a hierarchical social order in which he is either one-up or one-down, and conversations are negotiations for dominance. A woman engages the world as an individual in a network of connections, and conversations are negotiations for closeness. Tannen does not claim one approach is better than the other, but only that they are different, and if the genders understand this, they have a much easier time talking.

The quotation from C. S. Lewis is from his *The Four Loves* (London: Fontana Books, 1963), 111.

6

LIVING A COMMITTED RELATIONSHIP

People sometimes ask me how I can stand doing marriage counseling. It is true that many couples who come for counseling are not in good shape at all, and it is no fun to hear them go at one another. In fact, often they have arrived too late. The relationship is so deeply damaged that it is past salvaging. What miles they have traveled from the halcyon days of their first love!

When a relationship has not reached such a dire state, it is actually a pleasure to work with a couple. Then what I hear in their complaints and criticisms, their anger and tears, is essentially this: a man and a woman calling each other to growth. They are asking each other to stretch and become more caring human beings. That fits right into my own conception of what marriage, or any committed relationship, is all about, and I am happy to be there to support their efforts. I see marriage as a school for personal growth, a place to learn how to love. This is where its spirituality or inward significance lies. Every couple struggles. We come into marriage green, with little idea what committed love to spouse and children will demand of us. Shortcomings on both sides produce disappointment, irritation, cries of distress. Larger failings produce crises. All of it produces growth—if we work with it. If we are willing to listen to each other, we will hear some painful truth told and a call to personal growth. If we heed that, over time we will become much better persons than we were when we began. Marriage is no escape into bliss, but the free entry into a crucible of love in which both of us will be transformed. The key to success, and to all the satisfactions a good marriage yields, is to expect hard work from the outset, and to dedicate ourselves to the process.

Sam Keen says it well:

> Marriage is an aphrodisiac for the mature; a great yoga; a discipline of incarnate love; a task that stretches a man and a woman to the fullest; a drama in which a man and woman must gradually divest themselves of their archetypes and stereotypes and come to love each other as perfectly flawed individuals....If you consider marriage a lifelong romance, you are certain to be disillusioned. The shallowest of complaints is that marriage destroys romance. Of course it does. Marriage is designed to allow two people to fall out of love and into reality.

I would like to name nine ways we men are usually called upon to grow in the context of committed relationship. It is a fairly daunting set of challenges. But when we rise to meet them, home becomes a much happier place for everybody—our mates, our kids, ourselves. That is the reward. And a happy home launches everybody into much more enjoyable and fruitful engagements with the world.

1. *Get interested in your mate's feelings and in her life.* Listen to her. Listen attentively and long. She invariably regards this as the first or second most important expression of your love. Hers is usually a fairly rich inner life, and she takes it seriously. When she shares that with you, she is giving you herself. It is her way of loving, because she does not give this to everyone. Many a woman has to find another woman to give this to, when her husband does not value it. Sometimes she ends by giving it to another man. Talking about it to someone who cares

is not only how she gives herself, but also how she processes what is going on inside, getting more clarity about it and relieving some of its pressure.

There are three mistakes that we commonly make regarding this important communication.

- We half-listen from behind a newspaper or with one eye on the television.
- We tell her what she needs to do to solve her problem.
- We take her expressions of distress and frustration personally, and start arguing to defend ourselves.

All of this badly misses the mark. What she yearns for is something much simpler: Give me your attention, and listen to me with care. Try to understand. Just be with me where I now am.

That is all. And that is not really so difficult, once you catch on. The goal is understanding and empathy. Listen carefully, and try to imagine yourself in her shoes. Indicate that you understand and care—by your facial expression and the way you are attending, and by responses like, "I see what you mean." "I can understand why you feel that way." "That must be very difficult." "I've been there myself, and I know what you mean." (But don't go into your story.) Don't try to solve it unless she asks explicitly for advice. Just be with her in it. When you begin to share more of your own feeling-life, you will realize that this is exactly the kind of open receptiveness you want from her too.

2. *Keep tuned in to your mate, and anticipate her needs.* Do not presume that if your mate is not complaining everything is all right. It is far better to stay tuned in always, to ask her routinely how she is doing and what she needs, to foresee what she could use help with, and move in to lighten her load.

3. *Share what is going on inside you.* How much this means to women can hardly be overstated. This is for them the very essence of relationship, the core of the sense of being joined, the chief expression of intimacy. We explored how a man recovers his life of feeling and begins to share it in Chapter 3. Here, suffice it to repeat that every effort you make in this area for the one you love deepens the bond.

4. *Take responsibility for your health, physical and mental.* Why should a woman have to worry about a man's heart, his teeth, his prostate? Is he worrying about her teeth, her cervix, her breasts, urging her to get checkups? Should a woman have to live with a chronically unhappy man, worn down by his negativity, desperately pleading that he seek help? Should she have to live with a man who is in the grip of alcohol or drugs, is physically or verbally abusive, or is a workaholic at the expense of the most important relationships in his life? How can he be oblivious to all this, or so negligent of his own care?

It is only fair to ask that a man take responsibility for himself here. In the concrete, that means taking reasonable precautions against disaster (seat belt, helmet, condom, and so on), not imagining himself immune to ordinary dangers. It means taking care of his physical health—not smoking, drinking moderately, eating healthily, exercising several times a week, getting regular physical exams, and making his own appointment to see a doctor if he develops a symptom that does not go away. He also makes his own appointment to see a counselor if he finds himself chronically angry, depressed, or in the grip of problems to which he sees no solution.

Whether he lives or dies, and how he lives and dies, is a matter of the greatest consequence to those who love and depend on him. If he gets sick or has an accident, it is they who must suffer the financial impact and bear the burden of his care. If he is chronically unhappy or addicted, it is they who must put up with his severe personal limitations. No man is an island. We live in a web of relationships, in genuine interdependence. So it is not simply a question of how needy or how worthy of outside help you might consider yourself to be. It is also a matter of what love demands. Maybe you owe it to someone else.

5. *Learn to manage your anger.* There are two issues to attend to here. One is anger management. The other is searching for the deeper roots of anger. We looked at both in Chapter 3. Here, suffice it to repeat that while it is perfectly OK to *be* angry and to *name* your anger, it is not OK to *vent* anger, even at home. By venting, I mean hitting or grabbing someone, throwing something, hitting something, or using abusive language—in other words, letting it all hang out and becoming threatening. To get some sense of what that feels like to your mate and kids, imagine yourself with a man twice your size and three times stronger carrying on like that because he is angry at you. There are many other ways to express anger that are civil and respectful of others and much better suited to your getting whatever it is you seek.

If you are feeling angry a lot, probe that deeper unhappiness in yourself, find its cause, and do something about it. You will probably need the help of a therapist or close friend to dig down into it and begin to make some changes in your life. It may be hard work, but what a huge gift to yourself and those you love.

6. *Love your mate as she is.* A huge part of the act of love is loving the other person as is. It is difficult, because no one is quite as we would have them be. But that is really about us, isn't it? Inevitably, your mate has traits and habits that annoy you, and lacks traits you wish she had. Would that she loved sex more, or frugality, or entertaining your family. Would that she did not get depressed, or lose her temper, or put on weight. Now there is nothing wrong with asking for what you want.

Sometimes you get it, and asking is part of the dynamic of calling each other to growth. But suppose you have asked many times and nothing is changing. Then perhaps the time for acceptance has come. You will be more at peace, and she will certainly find life more pleasant, if you give up harping on these points and learn to love her as she is. Wouldn't you appreciate it if she loved you as you are? Think of all her virtues. And, if you are spiritually inclined, mull the mystery of how having to live with this particular set of qualities in her may be making more of a human being of you. The passive virtue of acceptance (with compassion) is no less a part of loving than all the active giving that love requires.

7. *Think of yourself as coresponsible for the relationship, the household, and the children.* This calls for an overhaul of the usual male mindset. Men naturally see themselves as providers, problem solvers, and repairmen, and they contribute generously to family life in these areas. This is great as far as it goes. But they tend to see themselves only as backup where cooking, cleaning, laundry, and taking care of the kids are concerned. They will do these things only when she is sick, or if she explicitly asks, and then they will feel as if they have done her a favor. The couple's social life and the getting of babysitters are other areas often assumed to be her responsibility.

This division of labor may have been fair when the man was sole breadwinner and the woman householder, though even then it leaves the kids with only a fraction of a father. But many families today have two breadwinners, and it is clearly unfair for the woman still to have primary responsibility for home and children besides her outside work. It is not enough for a man to be willing to do whatever is asked of him on an ad hoc basis, because this means that she still has to carry all the responsibility and do over half the work. Many a husband feels quite free to go off with his friends for an evening or even spend a weekend away. Can a wife presume the same liberty, and just assume that on relatively short notice he will be happy to cover everything in her absence?

And who is responsible for the relationship itself? Generally, women have carried this too, called attention to problems, and urged getting outside help when necessary. Men have simply responded, often minimally. And if she is not complaining, he thinks that everything is all right. But this means that he is neither listening to himself nor staying tuned in to her. If he were tuned in to her, he would know when she is not happy. If he were listening to himself, he would realize that he too feels dissatisfied sometimes with how the relationship is going. And if he were coresponsible for it, he would be the one to bite the bullet and say, "Honey, we need to talk about what is going on between us lately." He might even be the one leading the way to the therapist.

8. *Express appreciation and affection liberally.* This is the oil in the machinery of marriage. Everybody wants to feel loved, appreciated. Even you. When you are principal breadwinner, you like to hear a word of appreciation once in a while. So too if you tend the yard or keep the house in good repair. These are important ways that you express your love, and you do not like being taken for granted or taken advantage of. It is exactly the same with your mate. She too puts out in a variety of routines that can easily come to be taken for granted.

Don't let that happen. Say thank you a lot, even for the tasks of every day. Tell her regularly that you love her. Put your arm around her. Take her hand when you walk together. Embrace her when sex is the furthest thing from your mind. Tell her that she looks good, is intelligent, works hard, has a good sense of humor, has created a beautiful home, or whatever else about her that you appreciate and enjoy. Call her up. Bring her flowers. Remember and celebrate anniversaries and other special occasions. In these and other ways, let her know that she lives in your heart, and you really appreciate what you have.

One thing men commonly rue is the shortage of sex in their marriage. Of course, it helps when a woman understands that sex is one of the main ways a man feels loved, and that she might well see more loving behavior in him if she has sex with him on a regular basis. But a man needs to understand that a woman is built differently than he is. For her, sex does not come first. Closeness does. She does not withhold sex to punish him, as many a man believes. If she does not feel loved by him, she has no sexual feelings for him. That is where all this chapter's suggestions come in. It is these things—his listening to her, his sharing his inner life with her, his managing his anger, his coresponsibility for family life, his expressions of appreciation and affection for her—that make her feel cherished and cared for. When she feels loved, she feels sexual. She might even have sex with him when she is not feeling particularly sexy, because a cycle of mutual giving has been established.

9. *Stick with your commitment.* The value of a commitment is that it keeps us dedicated when we wonder if we want to be. It protects us against our natural tendency to backslide, to forget, to slip into fantasies of greener grass someplace else. A marriage goes through many stages over time. It requires adjustments, adaptations, new behavior. It has its seasons, and among them is winter. Why keep grappling with its challenges, accepting its disappointments, sweating through its hard times, contenting yourself with its ordinariness?

Because this is just life, whether here or anywhere else. Because there is so much that is good here, along with the struggles. Because if you leave her for someone else, you will just be exchanging one set of problems for another, and the new set might be worse than the old. Because you have built a lot together, and you will lose at least half of it if you split. Because your children will lose even more. And because wherever you go, *you* will still be there, which is a significant part of the problem. Because you become a human being precisely by sticking it out and seeing it through. Intimacy and commitment constitute a sort of crucible in which you are refined, purified, and slowly transformed. To make a break for it when the temperature rises is to settle for immaturity as a permanent way of being.

John Gottman, the University of Washington professor who has done extensive research on married couples, boils his findings down to a few essential differences between successful and unsuccessful couples.

> What I call "the masters of marriage" are individuals who are being kind to one another. They may raise difficult issues but they also soften them in a very considerate way. They frequently express appreciation. They communicate respect and love every day in numerous small ways. There are so many more positive exchanges in these relationships than those that are heading for divorce. These individuals show more affection for each other and they communicate greater interest in one another and use more humor. They scan their environment, looking for opportunities to say "thank you" rather than searching for mistakes the other person has made....The couples in our laboratory that turn out to have long happy marriages are responding to 96% of their partners' bids for attention by turning toward them with attention. That is a huge amount. In contrast, couples headed for divorce are responding only 30% of the time.

None of this is esoteric, though it does require awareness and practice. What strikes me is that it all amounts to practicing spirituality in marriage, that is, dedicating yourself to being genuinely loving, and working on a number of small virtues. Where the spirituality of marriage is concerned. I lay a lot of emphasis personally on the endless, unfolding dialogue. To me, it is the core of every marriage. Every issue of significance keeps turning up there. Be faithful to the dialogue and you will grow. Listen for the truth and submit to it. And always tell the truth, with love.

Reading Suggestions

Sam Keen, *Fire in the Belly* (New York: Bantam Books, 1992), is a thoughtful treatment of the whole spectrum of men's issues. His chapter on marriage and family is especially good. The quote above is from page 220.

John Gottman, *Why Marriages Succeed or Fail* (New York: Simon and Schuster, 1994), maintains that anger is a normal part of marital relating and does not necessarily harm a marriage. What does harm and eventually destroy a marriage are certain ways of expressing anger. These are criticism, contempt, defensiveness, and stonewalling. He elaborates on each of these and teaches better ways of communicating concerns. See also his *The Seven Principles for Making Marriage Work* (New York: Crown Publishers, 1999). The quotation from him on the keys to marital success is from an interview he gave in the *Newsletter of the Milton Erickson Foundation*, Vol. 21, No. 3, Winter 2001, p.1.

Neil Jacobsen, a behavioral marital therapist who published many books with programs for improved relating, ended his career by publishing one whose whole theme is mutual acceptance. See his *Reconcilable Differences* (New York: Guilford Press, 2000).

My wife and I have authored two books on marriage, which take up the core issues in much more detail than this chapter can. For couples starting out, see Kathleen Fischer and Thomas Hart, *The First Two Years of Marriage: Foundations for a Life*

Together (Mahwah, NJ: Paulist Press, 1983). For the whole span of marriage, see our *Promises to Keep: Developing the Skills of Marriage* (Mahwah, NJ: Paulist Press, 1991). Both integrate spirituality into a wealth of practical suggestions for success in the great venture.

7

BEING A DAD

My father was sole breadwinner for nine children. Through his labors our ship somehow stayed afloat financially, though, as you can imagine, a tight ship it was. From the perspective of adulthood, I can appreciate this part of his life, because I know now what it takes to go to work every day regardless of what else might be happening in your life. But my memories of him, which are warm, center on many smaller expressions of his love, acts of attentiveness of a more personal sort, which made me feel bonded to someone who was good and strong and fond.

He played catch with me in the driveway. And he hit me fly balls when we went to the park for Sunday picnics. He never shot baskets, though I went on to; nor did he ever toss a football, though I later did that too. He was not an athlete; he had grown up on a farm. He had no investment in my athletic prowess, never pushed me to excel. His motive was nothing other than love of the game, and of me. God knows, I treasured those moments with him. There is something about being with a man that is very exciting for a boy, if the man cares about him and shares what he has to give him. My dad and I played Ping-Pong too, on a table he had built in the basement. He was good at that game. He had a vicious serve and won almost every game for some years. When that changed, he still played, for as long as he felt he could "give me a game." When I was in the later grades, he taught me cribbage, and we played that through my high school years, usually at his invitation, amid his many responsibilities, in the middle of a Saturday or Sunday afternoon. These too were special moments. The pursuit is trivial. It is the attention, the companionship, the one-on-one.

I was his sidekick as he did his repairs around the house on Saturdays. I learned how to use tools, how to splice an electric wire, how to clear a drain and fix a toilet. We cleaned the basement and the garage, cleared the rain gutters, changed storm windows and screens, mowed the lawn, swept the walk. Of the work, I enjoyed very little, but I always relished being with him. And now I realize the immense value of the basic skills I learned from him.

A couple of times each summer, he would invite me to accompany him on his day's journey to different towns where he had sales calls to make. This was the best of all. It gave us a whole day together, a lot of it driving, with lunch in some restaurant he liked, or a picnic lunch in a park or near a stream. He had taught me to drive from the time I was little, first sitting on his lap and just steering. "Don't turn the corner before you get to it," he would say, as I learned that a car is quite a bit bigger than a bike. Then I learned to shift while he held the clutch in. Finally, my legs became long enough to do the footwork, and he moved over. So on these summer days (about 1950), a couple of years before I was of age, he would turn the driving over to me on the back roads of Wisconsin, and I took him where he wanted to go. He liked keeping up with his paperwork as we rode rather than having to do it later at home. And I was in my favorite place in the world, the driver's seat, next to my dad.

On the critical importance of this father-son relationship, psychologists Dan Kindlon and Michael Thompson offer this telling observation.

> When a grown man cries in therapy, it is almost always about his father....No matter how impossible a father may be, at the deepest level of his being a boy wants to love his father and to be known and loved by him.

Getting Involved

A father once remarked to me that it bothered him how his kids invariably brought their struggles to their mother, almost never to him. I knew his family fairly well, and it was evident that his wife knew the kids' lives far, far better than he did. She knew each of their teachers' names and had met them. She knew their friends and had spent enough time with them to have a sense of each. She knew when her kids' term papers were due, what their teams' records were, and who the best and worst players were. She knew how each of her kids felt about their scholastic and athletic abilities, what they enjoyed, what they found difficult or disliked. Dad had no such familiarity with his kids' worlds. How much easier and more natural for the kids to bring matters to Mom than to Dad. It was not a personality contest. It would take work to bring Dad up to speed. And would he be interested?

That is the first question here: Are you interested? Kids spell love T-I-M-E. You have to join them in their activities and invite them into yours. You teach them what you know and help them develop their own powers. You make it plain how important they are to you and how much you like being with them.

We can take it a notch higher. How would you like to be coparent rather than helper to your wife in this area? How would you like to be involved in the planning, the problem solving, and the caretaking on an equal basis? It would take a bite out of your time; something would have to give. But your kids would love it. And you just might too.

If you were not sure exactly how to begin a deeper joining, you could initiate an activity, give a compliment, or ask a question. For instance, you could ask: "If we could spend more time together, what would you like us to do?" You would soon be asking other questions, making observations, mulling solutions to difficulties. You would be ruminating on the struggles each child is going through at this time, encouraging them to keep talking about them, and being there to dialogue with them. You would share what you went through growing up, and what you learned from various experiences. And you would start learning all over again, brand new things, as this father suggests:

> If you let yourself learn from child-raising rather than just trying to control or perfect your children, they can lead you through all the stages of human development from the other side and help make you aware how men and women develop, how masculinity and femininity are taught and learned, and how to become a complete human being.

That is an interesting truth. Personal growth is never finished, and so parents are really in the same situation as their children. We used to think that by age eighteen, or perhaps twenty-one, a person was fully grown, and now it was just a matter of living adult life. We now conceive the entire lifespan as a learning and personal formation process. Many psychologists have mapped its stages. Recognizing this truth puts you and your kids on a much more level playing field, and makes you a more appealing figure. You are still learning, and are willing to say that you do not know the answer to many questions and dilemmas. You still make mistakes, and are willing to take responsibility for them, even apologizing when you offend.

Rich opportunities arise at the dinner table, as parents and children talk of the day's events. The evening meal is the family's pivotal institution, precisely because it is the daily occasion, over shared food and drink, for keeping in touch with each other's lives. All kinds of important issues lie just under the surface of the day's ordinary events—white and nonwhite, straight and gay, just and unjust, respect for authority and the limitations of those in authority, judgments, gender, work, suffering, negotiation and conflict-resolution, wealth and poverty and all the space in between, lifestyles, loss, happiness, boundaries, the meaning of life, individuality, to name just a few. A good question is often a great conversation starter, a question that occurs to you as you listen. It gets everybody thinking and talking. Then it is fun, everybody engaged, everybody learning and illuminating some aspect of the truth.

The kind of human being you form depends so much on the kind of human being you are and are still working on becoming. What do you model? What do you want to teach? Three dads try to put their conception of what is important into words.

> There are two qualities you should look for in your children: a sense of humor and whether they hang in there with a problem. If you see these two things, you needn't worry.

> The key to being a good father is providing love, schooling, and religion. If any one of these is missing in a home, you're bound to have trouble.

> Toss out or shoot the television set. If you read, the child will read. If you exercise, the child will exercise. If you work, the child will work. If you watch TV, the child will become the lazy slacker you seem to be.

What a challenge, this child-raising. What an opportunity. Why would you ask your wife to do it all? Or leave it to the schools? Yet you really have to think about this. Your time is limited, your loves many. How do you line up your priorities?

Guiding a Boy toward Manhood

Because our main focus in this book is on men, and men start as boys, let us look particularly at the task of raising boys.

How do we go about raising boys to be the sort of men that the human community needs them to be?

Dan Kindlon and Michael Thompson, psychologists who have made the raising and counseling of boys their particular study, offer two suggestions. Before you begin, form in your mind an image of the end-product, the kind of man you want your boy to become. Then direct your parenting efforts to the formation of that sort of man. And make "emotional literacy" central to your teaching. That is, teach a boy to recognize and respect all of his own feelings, and to be sensitive to the feelings of others. It is the lack of emotional literacy that makes so many men lonely, angry, and incapable of relating in any depth.

As far as models are concerned, some men are better than others, not just at particular pursuits, but in their quality as human beings. Which men do you admire? Which parts of yourself would you like to see replicated in your son? In which ways would you like him to be a better man than you? You will have many opportunities to read him stories or to watch movies with him. You can also bring him into contact with men whose qualities you would like him to experience. Some may be near at hand. And so, by example, exposure, and dialogue, you nudge him gently toward these sorts of self-realization.

It helps to be mindful of the peculiarities of boys' brain structure and hormones, which are quite different from girls', and require a different approach to training. The aggression center of a boy's brain is larger than that of a girl. And his main hormone, testosterone, the hormone of aggression and copulation, is twenty times more abundant in him than in her. So he is naturally much more aggressive and likely to engage in high-risk behaviors. On the other hand, he has much less progesterone, the bonding hormone, than a girl has. So you have to put more energy into teaching him how to bond, that is, to be empathetic, appreciative, and sensitive, and to be moral, which is essentially a matter of respecting the rights and feelings of others. And you have to put a great deal of effort into teaching him how to harness and channel his aggressive and sexual energies.

What about physical punishment? Should you hit him? Some men just hit, no questions asked. And some really lay it on. But research shows that this form of discipline, particularly if it is severe, is harmful. It ruins the relationship between father and son, and it fails to teach much more than fear. The boy remembers the pain, but not the moral lesson. There are any number of other consequences you can use for bad behavior that serve the same deterrent function. And your most important task when your son does something wrong is to help him see what makes it wrong.

How do you teach a boy respect for girls as his equals? Home is the primary school for this. You teach it in how you treat your wife and daughter(s), and how you insist that he treat his mother and his sister(s). Our culture is sexist, and his exposure to large doses of that will manifest in some of the things he says and does in his dealings with girls and women. There will be many teaching moments here.

Earlier, I called attention to that pivotal moment in a boy's life when he begins receiving those "masculine" messages about the requisite hardness he must show if he is to be a man. This is reverse sexism, another straightjacket. You have a crucial role to play here, first, in not giving him such messages yourself, and second, in helping him deal with the messages and behavior coming at him from other boys and men. Here lies the opportunity to impart a much richer, more balanced notion of what it means to be a man. You do have to teach him to be strong, to stand his ground, to defend himself. But he must not lose his capacity to feel and to be sensitive to the feelings of others. In the "culture of cruelty" that most boys move in and have to navigate, he will feel fear, be hurt, feel inadequate. There is no point in denying these feelings. He can learn when to show them, when not, when to express them, when not. But he need not learn to be cruel, to "pass on the sting." Nor need he become so hardened that he can no longer feel much of anything except anger, losing his capacity to relate to the many people he will meet who are no threat to him at all, who might, in fact, wish to be his friends. Besides helping him preserve and develop his emotional literacy, adults, both parents and teachers, can help boys also by intervening to break up this culture of cruelty, insisting on a moral code of respect for one another. Without that, boys can really damage each other in ways very difficult to heal.

Your daughter needs a different but equally crucial message from you about what it means to be female. She needs to hear from you that female is every bit as good as male, that she too is both intelligent and strong, and that she can dream big about what her life in the world might be. You grieve with her over the sexism that still exists in our society, and you struggle with her and others to overcome it.

Adolescence

What should a father say to his kids when they enter adolescence? I often find my own answer to a hard question like this by asking: What messages would I like to have heard from my dad, or my mom, as I entered that difficult stage of life? You might try that question on yourself, and let it be your guide. What would you like someone to have said to you about sexuality, for instance—that huge fact of life at any age, seizing our attention with particular force in adolescence? How often a kid is left alone with all this, except for Mom telling a girl she is going to start having periods and how to deal with them, and Dad possibly telling his son that he better not get anybody pregnant. Not only is there a dearth of information and ethical guidelines, but often enough when puberty comes to a daughter, many a father who had enjoyed free physical exchange with her through the years without any inappropriateness, suddenly pulls away from her, no longer touching her at all. What message does this send, and where does it leave her? She really could use some help with all this in the form of dialogue.

How might a father be a better participant in these exciting developments in his son's and daughter's lives? It will not be in a single speech, but in a series of statements and questions over time, hopefully opening dialogues. Something about your own adolescence would be a good place to start—the fears and uncertainties, the excitement, the curiosity, the messages from other kids, your parents' help or lack of help. Then something of your view of sexuality now, on the basis of a lot more experience. That might include your appreciation of its generative power, the wonder of bringing a child into the world when the conditions are right. You can frame the pleasure of sex, its power to form a unique bond between two people, and its generativity as wonderful gifts for which to be grateful. You can talk to your son about how strong the male sexual urge is, and how difficult yet necessary it is to harness that energy and integrate it into responsible loving. You can tell him you are still working at that today, as the male sexual urge remains restless even when one is committed. You will probably have to spend a lot of time trying to get across the truth that teenagers are not ready for full sexual relationships, and why that is, even if some teens are into it. You try to teach him respect for girls and women not just in words but in how you relate to them yourself. You try to keep this dialogue open as your son moves year by year through puberty and into young adulthood. These are hard things for most of us to talk about. We have to think deeply about it, seize our opportunities, take some risks. There is one compelling motive: Our kids need it. If we don't do it, who will?

What about your daughter? Here too, a couple of clear, loving messages from Dad can be invaluable. The first is appreciation and celebration, of her developing into a woman, of her carrying in her body now the amazing power of forming and bringing a new human being to birth and of nurturing it. There is something of the Great Mystery reflected in that. You can also teach her about male sexuality, especially that male sexuality is a powerful force in a boy that comes unintegrated. When a boy comes on to her sexually, it does not necessarily mean love, and she has to be clear and strong in taking care of herself, setting limits, and calling the boy to authenticity. Only over time and through struggle does a boy integrate his sexuality into responsible loving.

What about the sexual feelings your daughter might stir in you? This is actually quite common and no cause for alarm. She is attractive, and your sexual energy has a life of its own, as you know. You have your own integration project to keep working at, so that your expressions of affection toward all women are authentic, responsible, and appropriate. You can continue to put your arm around your daughter and give her hugs. Show her what healthy male sexuality looks like even as you educate her about its unhealthy manifestations.

Both your son and daughter deserve abundant knowledge about sexual relating: especially about how pregnancy happens and how sexual diseases get transmitted. Our culture is full of sexual stimuli, and we have to work closely with our kids to help them navigate its waters. Some particular suggestions might be helpful. Dating one-on-one is best held off until at least age sixteen, there being many other ways for boys and girls to bond and enjoy each other's company before that. When a dating relationship begins, we want to meet the date, and want our child to meet the date's parents too. We want to know where they will be when they go out, and hold the line on when they must be home. We stress that sex and love are moral issues, with both parties sharing the responsibility. We teach our son to accept no from a girl, and both son and daughter to talk with their partner every step of the way as physical intimacy develops. We teach abstinence as the course we strongly prefer, trying to give persuasive reasons for that. But, with a sense of realism, particularly as our kids get older, teach contraception as well. We tell them that no matter what question arises, we will be there to help them find an answer.

Though we have spent some time on the topic of sexuality, it is by no means the only issue for a boy in adolescence. Accepting himself, belonging yet maintaining his own identity, mastering his aggressive instincts, succeeding academically, driving responsibly, beginning to think toward his future work, and coming to sensible positions on his use of alcohol and drugs are other major ones. The adolescent boy needs his parents as much as he ever did, only in different ways now. And often enough, he is difficult to deal with. One experienced dad remarks:

> Don't pull back from loving your children during adolescence just because they pull back from you and your efforts to control, protect, or fix them. It is just when they hate you most that they most need your steady, reliable love.

Dan Kindlon and Michael Thompson's seven principles for raising a boy might serve as a summary of our reflections on being good dads to our sons.

1. Give boys permission to have an internal life, approval for the full range of human emotions, and help in developing an emotional vocabulary so that they may better understand themselves and communicate more effectively with others.
2. Recognize and accept the high activity level of boys and give them safe boy places to express it.
3. Talk to boys in their language—in a way that honors their pride and their masculinity. Be direct with them; use them as consultants and problem solvers.

4. Teach boys that emotional courage *is* courage, and that courage and empathy are the sources of real strength in life.
5. Use discipline to build character and conscience, not enemies.
6. Model a manhood of emotional attachment.
7. Teach boys that there are many ways to be a man.

Some adults I have seen in counseling, both men and women, have lamented the fact that their parents gave them too little guidance toward careers. As a result, they still feel unsure of themselves in the world, whatever they may be doing. What they wish that they had gotten is help in identifying their strengths, affirmation for what they did well, and the extending of lines from there into possible career options. It is, of course, quite wrong to steer a child toward a particular career, for example, going into ministry, taking over the family business, becoming the doctor or lawyer or professor that Mom or Dad always wished they had become. A child's gifts and inclinations have to be the starting point. Encourage them to keep developing these, and keep a dialogue going with them about possible flowerings.

As if raising children were not challenge enough, about the time our labors are finished there, our parents begin needing our care. Here too, the tradition has been that this is women's work, and so our sisters take care of it, or our wives who also have their own parents to attend to. Our sole responsibility has been to contribute money if necessary. This is another arrangement in which women have carried too much of the burden, and men's capacity for caring and nurture has been undersold.

A friend of mine feels guilty to this day that he did not spend time with his dying mother who had cancer, but there is nothing he can do now. His mother had no daughters, just two sons. My friend understood perfectly well that all his mother would have wanted was that he spend time with her, sit with her, talk with her a little. He did not do it. His reason? He felt inadequate. He was afraid she would ask him questions about the meaning of it all that he would not be able to answer. He was afraid to be that close to her pain, because there was nothing he could do to take it away. So he avoided the scene, and she died without family around. One does not need to be God to sit with a dying parent. One needs only to be there and to care. And it is a privilege to render the little services one can—a drink of water, a chip of ice, an adjustment of the pillow, a holding of the hand.

Though we have ended with a thought on our role in caring for aging parents, our main focus has been on parenting our children, and the message is this. A man's children clearly need (and want) him to get involved in their parenting. His sons need him particularly, and the fashioning of a good man begins with the dawn of his consciousness. We have no more important work in our lives. In his *Fire in the Belly,* Sam Keen expresses himself strongly on the need for men to get involved.

> The only revolution that will heal us is one in which men and women come together and place the creation of a rich family life back in the center of the horizon of our values. A letter I got recently from a woman makes the point. "Perhaps the real shift will come when men fully realize, in the gut and not just in the head, that they are equally responsible, with women, for the creation, nurturing, and protection of children—that children are not simply sex objects, ego trips, or nuisances, but their first responsibility—before war, money, power, and status." (p. 226)

Reading Suggestions

The statements from various dads are from that wonderful collection of men's thoughts on important topics in Joe Kita, ed., *The Wisdom of Our Fathers* (Emmaus, PA: Rodale Books, 1999), pp. 105, 110, 111, 118, 119.

Michael Thompson, *Speaking of Boys: Answers to the Most-asked Questions about Raising Sons* (New York: Ballantine, 2000), and Michael Gurian, *The Good Son: Shaping the Moral Development of Our Boys and Young Men* (New York: Tarcher/Putnam, 1999), are two good books by experienced psychologists on the art of raising boys.

Dan Kindlon and Michael Thompson, *Raising Cain: Protecting the Emotional Life of Boys* (New York: Ballantine, 1999), another fine book, has "emotional literacy" as its theme and is the source of the seven principles. The quote above on page 65 is from pages 94–95 in *Raising Cain.*

Geoffrey Canada, *Reaching Up for Manhood: Transforming the Lives of Boys in America* (Boston: Beacon Press, 1998), tells of one man's work in rehabilitating boys who did not get what they needed at home. It is a good resource for those struggling with particularly difficult sons.

8

FINDING YOUR TRUE SELF

One of the core tasks for each of us, women and men, is to find our true self. It is not as easy as it looks. We might be unaware that there is such a thing. Or we might think that we found it long ago and have been living out of it all along. But that is to discount the powerful shaping influences of family, culture, and church, not to mention advertising, all of them conspiring to make us what they would have us be, making it hard to hear what we more truly are.

A businessman's wife asked another businessman to talk with her husband, who was miserable most of the time. The man confessed that he felt like a failure. Once a year he gathered with business friends, and they talked about their exploits, earnings, and the toys they had bought. He found himself consistently below average and felt very small. The friend, in his own line of business, had risen to the top of his field, wielded power, enjoyed affluence, and experienced everything that brought. He had moved on now to a life much more meaningful to him, working less and earning less, putting his time now where his heart was, with humanitarian causes he believed in and with family and friends. And so he was in an excellent position to point out to this man that he was living his life by someone else's standard, and that it was time to come home to himself. What was really important to him? What gave him satisfaction and joy? What did he want to do with his life? To questions like these, the man had never given much thought.

But that is the critical issue for each of us. What do I most want to do with my life? What kind of person do I most want to be? It is up to me, and my life is at stake.

Joseph Campbell used to say, "Follow your bliss," drawing on the wisdom of age-old myths. Carl Jung talked often about the importance of finding your true self and living your destiny. Jesus put the matter in the form of a question: "What does it profit you to gain the whole world if you lose your very self (soul)? Indeed, what can you offer in exchange for your self (soul)?" (Mark 8:36–37. The Greek word *psyche* in Jesus' saying means either *soul* or *self*, that is, the inner core of the person.)

You have probably heard the phrase "finding your own voice." If you listen to the first two symphonies of Beethoven, you will hear Mozart in them, Beethoven's eminent predecessor. With his Third Symphony, Beethoven has found his own voice, and Mozart is heard no more. Then it was Brahms's turn. You will not hear Beethoven in Brahms's First Symphony. But so imposing was Beethoven that Brahms set his First Symphony aside after writing just two movements—set it aside for fourteen years before he found the courage to take it up again. How much poorer the world would be without Brahms's four symphonies, different from, but in no way inferior to, Beethoven's nine. Picasso once remarked, "When I was a kid, I drew like Michelangelo. It took me years to learn to draw like a kid." To draw like a kid is, of course, to let out your own spontaneous creativity, and draw from there.

Going Inside to Find Your Direction

How do you find your own voice, your true self? You have to listen to what is going on inside you. You have to start going inside instead of outside. Do an inner probe several times a day and see if you can answer four questions in the various situations in which you find yourself: What do you feel? What do you think? What do you need? What do you want?

- What do you feel? Your feelings are an elaborate information system, telling you how you are in given situations. Knowing how you feel and sharing your feelings effectively with others are the keys both to creating deeper relationships and to getting what you need and want.
- What do you think? Developing your own perspectives requires accurate information and serious reflection. But if you do not have your own ideas and the courage of your convictions, you can hardly be said to be living out of your own center. Letting the media, your peers, or the polls tell you what to believe is a sellout of the self and an abdication of adult responsibility.
- What do you need? You might, as a man, prefer not to need anything, to be completely self-sufficient, or at least not to admit that you have any needs. But you do. Sometimes you need a break. Sometimes a little appreciation. Sometimes you need help. Or companionship. Or an apology. Here again, it is a matter of identifying the felt need, and then being man enough to ask for it.
- What do you want? Your wanting has various levels of seriousness. There is "I would like," and "I feel like," and even "I wish." These are all interesting and informative but superficial. It is the deeper levels of wanting that tell you who you really are. It is from deep down that, for example, you long to love, to do the right thing, to contribute something of value before you die. It is from there also that each of us, uniquely, finds the attractions that shape our peculiar life direction. This wholehearted wanting is the only sound basis of motivation. A blend of feeling and thinking, it has the power to sustain us over the long haul, through the inevitable difficulties of any major

enterprise. Getting in touch with this and living from it are obviously matters of the highest importance.

There is an important corollary for those who seek to do God's will. Many a person asks: What does God want me to do with my life? Or what does God want me to do about this particular matter? Well, when you have found what you most deeply want to do, you will have found God's will for you. God's will for you is already planted in the soil of your selfhood. The heart of the Christian faith is that God is good and loves us. That means life is a gift, and God is for us. God's creative wish for us, then, might be compared to what our parents, if they truly love us, also clearly want: that we flower into the fullness of our personhood and enjoy the life which flows from there, whatever form(s) that might take.

If you are addicted to alcohol or drugs, you will have trouble finding your true self. You are anesthetized. You are not listening to yourself, but drowning yourself out. You have also arrested your personal growth. When you get free, you will have to resume the task of your personal development at the psychological age that you were when you started drugging yourself instead of grappling with the challenges of life. That grappling is the only path to becoming a mature person.

If you want to know yourself and find the divinity within, you have to spend time alone. You have to turn off the television and the music, close your eyes sometimes and go inside. You have to read things that make you think. You have to walk. You might even make a retreat now and then, if you can get away for a few days. A retreat always gets you in deeper touch with yourself and makes you reflect on what you are doing and what life is really all about.

If you can manage a walk by yourself on a Saturday or Sunday afternoon, there are three questions you might profitably ask yourself. What is bothering me? What am I longing for? Who could use my help? These are, obviously, three quite diverse inquiries.

• The first gets you looking at the rumblings and grindings deep down, the ones that work drowns out, the ones that make their presence felt unbidden in your angry driving or your snapping at your mate or kids. If you do not get in touch with what is bothering you, how can you do anything about it? Is it your work? Your marriage? Some other relationship? Your own relentless inner critic?

• The second question, about your longings, is another depth probe, but into the area of positive energies. Your longings are the same as your deepest wanting, and show you the direction in which you need to move. Perhaps you long for a mate. Perhaps you long for more time with your children, or for more real closeness with your wife. Perhaps you yearn for work that would better use your talents and give you more satisfaction. Perhaps your longings are for something deeper still, for more closeness with the Mystery that lies at the core of your existence. Or you may already be in touch with the One in whom you live, move, and have your being, and your yearning is to find ways to bring that spirituality into your work place—for instance, in the attitude you bring to your endeavors, the values that govern your choices, the ways you might try to change the climate of your work place for everyone's benefit. Listening to your longings will help you get your life on its proper course, for, as we have seen, the clues to your destiny lie within you.

• The third question, about who could use your help, directs your attention outside yourself to the larger context in which you are embedded. In the end, you are made for love, for the giving and receiving of love. Sometimes you think that happiness lies in having more things and enjoying more pleasures. But before long you discover that this does not satisfy the soul. Meanwhile, all around you people are suffering, some in the direst need. Who needs you? Whom can you help? What do they need? Why don't you extend yourself to give something to at least some of them? When you begin to move in that direction, you begin to feel reasons to live.

Though the emphasis in this section has been mainly on going inside to find our true self, it is evident that we find significant parts of ourselves also by being with and listening to others. We develop in relationship. We also come to know parts of ourselves only in interaction with others. We might not be aware of what our gifts are, for instance, until someone else calls them to our attention. So our search for the self and our developing of that self are not solitary pursuits, even though they involve inwardness. We are essentially social and become ourselves in relationship. Family, friends, teachers, fellow workers, and mentors have very important roles to play in our becoming.

What about "I Should"?

People sometimes express the fear that if they just do what they *want* to do, they will behave very badly. We have already distinguished "I want" from "I feel like." But what about "I should"? Are we just tossing that out?

When we are small, adults are constantly telling us what we should and should not do. We usually comply, either to please them or to avoid punishment. That is how we build up our set of "shoulds." As we become adults, we develop the capacity to make our own judgments about the inculcated program. As we review and assess the values embedded in that program, we endorse many of them and reject others. Now we are in a different situation. Now we are honest because we *choose* to be honest; it is our own owned value. Now we get the work done first and then play, neither to please parents nor to avoid punishment, but because we have embraced that as a genuine value. This means that the old "should" has been personally assimilated as an adult "want." Other "shoulds," by contrast, are now unconvincing, for example, certain religious programs, or the principle that whatever is worth doing is worth doing well, or the idea that the best thing you can do with money is to save it. We are no longer convinced of the value of these "shoulds" our parents or others lived and taught.

Of course, not everyone goes through this mature reevaluation. There are quite a few adults who have no confidence in their own judgment or experience, and would rather live under authority than assume their own proper autonomy. They persist in preferring to be told what is right and wrong, what is true and false. They may even canonize a certain source of authority, effectively eliminating all doubt. This surrender to authority frees them from the risks of taking responsibility for their own lives, but it exacts a high price. It keeps them in perpetual childhood and leaves them vulnerable to exploitation.

The point for our present purposes is that the mature person lives from his "wants" rather than from a program of extrinsic "shoulds." How does this play out where important choices are concerned?

A man in his mid-forties came for counseling. He had been married some twenty years. Lately, he found himself thinking of leaving his marriage. He had never really been happy, it seemed, but he had been raised with a strong sense of duty and so had stayed with it. His sense of responsibility to the children had been a big factor in that. But now the children were launched, and the rumblings of his discontent grew louder.

His wife was a good person, he recognized, but he had never felt loved by her for who he was. Though he still respected and cared about her, his love had waned. Yes, he acknowledged the value of fidelity and knew that his wife would strongly prefer to remain married, but his heart was not in it anymore. All his energy was flowing outward now, toward liberation and some kind of new life. He did not know what shape that life would take, not even whether he would find someone with whom to share it. But it was time. When he told his wife, she was stunned.

I believe in marital permanence as a great value, for many reasons. I told him so, but I acknowledged that this would not decide the question for him. He had to decide it. And he had to go with his heart, because over the long haul nothing else would work. So the question I put to him was: When you consider everything, what is it you most deeply want to do?

Wholehearted wanting is the only thing that sustains us over the long haul. If this man sets aside what he really wants and stays with his wife simply from a sense of obligation, miserable and dying inside, what good is he even to her? His body is there, but his heart is not. He is in the chair, but he is depressed and has anger smoldering inside him. In fact, his wife had the good sense to tell him this. Though she strongly believed in the possibilities of their marriage—fresh possibilities—she did not want him to stay unless he really wanted to be there.

If we reflect on his situation in light of the ideas we have been considering, we can see that this man makes his choice to marry when he is young and knows neither himself nor his wife very well. But he chooses what he wants. As their relationship unfolds and he matures, he discovers more of himself and more of her, and finds that there are large gaps in the relationship. He considers leaving her, but chooses to stay for the sake of the children. This, it seems to me, is an example of an integrated "should": He "wants" to stay for the sake of the children. But when the children are raised, he can no longer see a compelling value in staying. Neither of them is happy, and what had held them together for many years is gone. A new value has become compelling—the freedom to be himself and live the life he wants. He does not believe he can do that in this relationship. So he leaves and embarks on a new life.

It does not always go that way. A man sixty-one years old has been a priest since he was thirty, but is miserable. He goes to his superior and tells him his plight. "I haven't been happy in this life for many years. I wish I had left long ago. It is too late now. There is no way I can get a new job and support myself. I'm just plain trapped." His superior is wise and says to him, "There is no value whatsoever in your going on as an unhappy priest, because an unhappy priest is no good to anyone. If money is your only concern, let's do this. We will give you so much money a month until you die, enough for you to live on. If you want to go, you are free to go." The priest is flabbergasted. He never expected this. He says that he needs to think now.

After a few days, he returns. "I've decided to stay," he says. "But I stay a happy man. I no longer feel trapped. Thank you for your generous offer to me. When I thought about going, I realized that there is a lot I love about being a priest, and I think I've been a good priest and can continue to be. But I am going to be a priest now because I *choose* to be a priest, and that makes all the difference." This man, who for years had done what he thought he *had* to do, was suddenly given the freedom to do whatever he wanted. And he discovered, paradoxically, that what he wanted was exactly what he was doing, but the basis had changed dramatically.

There is a world of difference between a "should" and a "want," not always in the content, but in the feeling. You are probably familiar with that difference. Your body knows it. A "should" feels as if it comes from your head, or from outside into your head. It is a force, but it feels like a force from outside. A "want" arises from inside your loins. It too is a force, but it might better be called an energy, and it feels as if it is your own. A quiet excitement often accompanies it, even when what you are choosing will entail struggle and suffering.

But let us come back to the moral issue. Isn't doing what you want essentially selfish? In the two cases above, wasn't the first man selfish, the second man unselfish, in their choices? I do not think so. There is plenty of self-interest in the second man's choice. And there is plenty of courage in the first man's; in many ways, it would be easier for him to stay. By leaving, he incurs his wife's wrath, the condemnation of his children, and the disapproval of significant others, not to mention large financial losses. And he may end up alone.

If we examine them closely, we will find that there is a measure of self-interest even in our most "selfless" choices. Loving others generously, for instance, is gratifying to us in some ways. There is nothing wrong with that. Our motives are often a mix of many ingredients. And a proper love of self is part of Jesus' great commandment: Love your neighbor as yourself. Jesus *presumes* that you love yourself and pushes you to love your neighbor in the same way. Yes, it is possible to go overboard in pursuing your own interests, especially if you hurt others. But it is also possible to go overboard in taking care of others, neglecting your own legitimate needs and wants. That dishonors you. This latter tendency is a real temptation for good people.

So the process developed in the chapter is this: Find your true self. Trust that self. Dare, humbly, to be that person in the world. Each of us is born to bring a unique and irreplaceable sound to the great cosmic symphony.

Reading Suggestions

Parker Palmer writes helpfully of the search for your true self in his *Let Your Life Speak* (San Francisco: Jossey-Bass, 2000).

I develop the thesis that God's will for us is found inside our own deepest wanting in my book on spiritual guidance, *The Art of Christian Listening* (Mahwah, NJ: Paulist Press, 1980), as well as in my book *Hidden Spring: The Spiritual Dimension of Therapy* (Minneapolis, MN: Augsburg Fortress Press, 2002).

Leo Rock, SJ, *Making Friends with Yourself* (Mahwah, NJ: Paulist Press, 1991), is a very helpful book both for finding your true self and for befriending the self that you find.

9

TAKING YOUR PLACE IN THE WORLD

A man's work is a very important part of his life. His self-respect is closely tied to his having a job and feeling good about telling others what he does. If he has a family, he regards supporting them financially as his first responsibility and one of the main expressions of his love. Some men identify with their work and think of what they earn as the chief mark of their success or failure in life. When a man is unemployed, he often becomes depressed. Sometimes he avoids going out altogether because he fears the inevitable question: What do you do? I have counseled a few men who were already so wealthy from their parents' business that they did not need to work. They suffered role-identity crises and floundered in the world. I have counseled men who were employed very lucratively, but hated their work and so were habitually depressed.

Here I invite you to reflect on your work. There are several important questions. How do you figure out what you are supposed to do? How do you balance work with family life? What is "success"? And how might you go about spiritualizing your work?

Do What You Love

Your choice of the work you will do is one of the weightiest of your life. Not that you have to get it right the first time, nor that you cannot make adjustments or even make complete career changes later on. Many people today will pursue several lines of work in their lifetime. But your work is so central to your sense of yourself in the world, and it takes up so much of your time and energy that this very important choice really deserves some reflection. When a man says to me, "I hate my job," I always respond, "Then you'd better make a change soon."

A man who had been laid off from a job in advertising told me that he almost accepted a position in the software industry with one of the corporate giants. "I knew when I interviewed that I did not like the atmosphere. Everything I had heard about that world turned me off, and when I was there too I felt creepy. But when they offered me a job, I was flattered that they wanted me, and I nearly took it." I can understand the feeling flattered, the salary offer, and the prospects for upward mobility in such a corporation. I can also understand his eagerness to get back to work. But this man was not listening to himself. In every step of the process, his body was telling him he did not want to be there. What possible sense would it have made for him to take this job and be miserable in it from beginning to end? Just to tell his friends he had a job, and could flash the corporate name on his business card? Is that what success is? Back comes Jesus' question: "What does it profit a man to gain the whole world if he suffer the loss of his *self*?" (Mark 8: 36–37)

In *What Color Is Your Parachute?*, a workbook for those seeking to figure out what kind of work to do, Richard Bolles offers two main criteria: What are you good at? And what do you love doing? This may sound like common sense, but I doubt that these criteria could be improved upon. The feedback you have received from others over the years is certainly part of the data here. In choosing your work, these two basic guidelines certainly take precedence over salary scale, perks, and whatever other people might think about your station in the world. Marsha Sinetar takes that second criterion a step further, and her thought is entirely conveyed in the title of her book: *Do What You Love, the Money Will Follow.* (She knows that what you love will almost certainly be something that you are good at.)

You do have to figure out the practicalities. What you love may not pay the bills, at least for the lifestyle to which you have become accustomed. You may have to settle for doing it on the side, at least for a while. Or you might change your lifestyle. You may have to take a pay cut to start with. You may have to go back to school to make the shift. You may have to take out a loan. But if you think long term, the costs are usually worth it. A little story from the wisdom tradition offers a perspective.

> The philosopher Diogenes was eating lentils for supper. He was seen by the philosopher Aristippus who lived comfortably by flattering the king. Said Aristippus, "If you would learn to be subservient to the king you would not have to live on such garbage as lentils." Said Diogenes, "If you had learnt to live on lentils you would not have to flatter the king."

Sometimes it only takes an adjustment in the line of work you are already in. I know a couple of attorneys who, after some years at the profession, began to feel discontent. One moved into direct legal advocacy for the poor, the other into the legalities of probation work with troubled youth. That is all it took, and they were happy again. I know a physician who began to see a need for structural changes in the way the medical profession delivers health care, and went to school to learn management, then took a job in management to work for change.

Balancing Work with the Rest of Your Life

So central is his work to a man that he sometimes drowns in it. He loses the distinction between his work and his life, between his work and his identity. They become fused into one.

We call these men *workaholics,* and there is accuracy in the term because there is an addictive quality to such a man's driveness. He seems in the grip of something. He is no longer at the wheel of his own car; he is a passenger. To some of these men, even taking a vacation is unthinkable.

All of the addictions—alcohol, drugs, sex, gambling, work, consumerism—represent in part an attempt to fill the empty space inside with something that can never fill it, because only God can. But they are not quite that simple either. There are biochemical factors, sometimes a desperate attempt to push out depression, and sometimes a search for love. But whenever any addiction gets this far out of balance in a person's life, the whole matter needs to be searched out for the causes that drive it, and something more appropriate put in place of the addictive substance.

Your work is not your life. It is two things: making your contribution to the world, and earning the money on which you need to live. If you can maintain this perspective, you will take your work seriously but not get lost in it. You will still have a life, which you certainly deserve—friends, family, the activities you enjoy, and possibly some other ways you like to contribute, such as coaching or other forms of volunteering.

We saw in the last chapter how important a father is to his kids. If you are married, this has to be a huge consideration. So is the most important relationship in your life, that with your wife, which will outlive the child-raising years. Work and family both deserve your dedication.

I know a man with five children whose heart is with his family. His work is merely instrumental. Providing for so large a family takes a good bit of money, and so he has had to set aside what he would much rather do—run a bookstore—and keep his job as a foreman in industry. The work is stressful. Every evening on his way home, he parks and sits quietly for ten or fifteen minutes. He "decontaminates" himself from the stresses of his workday, thus making a transition. He prepares himself mentally to arrive home and be available as a calm and loving presence to those who are most important to him. He does not want to enter that scene harried, preoccupied, or irritable. What a concept. What care. And what a sacrifice, to set aside what he would rather do in favor of providing more generously for his family. First came the job, then the kids in pretty rapid succession, and so the necessity, despite discontent, of retaining the job for financial reasons. He is not exactly doing what he loves. But he has put his work energies into the service of what he loves.

There are other situations where a wife knows how important her husband's career is to him, and she supports him in it by doing with less of him. She is willing to carry most of the responsibilities of domestic life, enjoying time together as it comes. Sometimes a woman's career has that kind of importance for her, and her husband supports it with whatever sacrifices he has to make. There are many ways of working out the tension between career and family.

One of the most interesting couples I know have done a straight role reversal. What unites them is a deeply felt call to care for children. After having a few of their own, they were moved to reach out, and have gradually adopted several orphaned children from various poor countries. The house is filled with life—and challenge. The woman is a business consultant and has far more earning power than her husband. He is a gentle, loving, nurturing man, even more gifted in dealing with children than she is. She is the breadwinner. He is the homemaker. When this family goes out to a restaurant, they catch a few glances.

Sam Keen, musing on his own career, offers a retrospective that raises a question.

> I don't know who I would be without the satisfaction of providing for my family, the occasional intoxication of

> creativity, the warm companionship of colleagues, the pride in a job well done, and the knowledge that my work has been useful to others. But there is still something unsaid, something that forces me to ask questions about my life that are, perhaps, tragic: In working so much have I done violence to my being? How often, doing work that is good, have I betrayed what is better in myself and abandoned what is best for those I love? How many hours would have been better spent walking in silence in the woods or wrestling with my children? Two decades ago, near the end of what was a good but troubled marriage, my wife asked me: "Would you be willing to be less efficient?" The question haunts me. (*Fire in the Belly*, p. 67)

So what is "success"? To my mind, it starts from living out of your personal center, "following your bliss," as Joseph Campbell puts it, that bliss unique to each of us. You live the life that makes best sense to you, free from concern for what others might think about it. You balance work with the other components of a complete life—important relationships (whether you have a family or not), satisfying activities, the life of your body, your emotions, your mind, your spirit. Your identity lies in no single one of these components, but in the unique way you combine them and put your personal stamp on each.

The Spirituality of Work

Spirituality is often presented as a separate activity, something over and above what you spend the rest of your life doing. For example, earlier I talked about meditating, taking a walk by yourself, making a retreat. They all require taking time out. But is there a spirituality for people who cannot seem to find the time to take out, a spirituality to be lived right in the midst of the hurly-burly? Might there be something inherently spiritual about work itself, or, for that matter, about home life? It seems that there is. Jesus lived and worked in the thick of the world, with only occasional time-outs to be alone. Perhaps there is a way even for the busiest and least pious of us to make work itself holy, depending on how we approach it.

How might you bring more spirituality to your work place, whether you are the CEO or the lowest-paid worker? Are there ways of being and acting that reflect a spiritual dedication, without disrupting the flow of work or offending anyone? Actually, there are many.

You can surround yourself with "sacred objects." I mean photos of your family, for whom you are working, photos of other people who are mentors or models for you, and other objects that remind you of larger perspectives and deeper values whenever your eye falls on them.

You could accept your imperfection and relax more. The very best fielders in baseball, after playing the game at the highest level for years, still can't get all the errors out of their game. You are in the same situation, and so are your fellow workers and the people with whom you do business. Accepting that is the beginning of peace.

In fact, it might enable you to appreciate your colleagues more. Everybody, even the person who cleans the workspace by night, is making a contribution, and everybody likes to know that it is noticed and appreciated. Thank them. I have counseled many people who have longed for just an occasional word of praise from their bosses, and never gotten it. The boss seems to notice them only when there is a problem. Liberal doses of appreciation really oil the machinery of work. And what you sow, you reap.

You can build community. Welcome the newcomer. Empathize with the person who is going through something difficult in his or her personal life. Reach out to the lonely and the less sure. Remember birthdays. Refrain from joining in criticism and tearing people down. Oppose sexism in all of its manifestations, and do what you can to promote mutually respectful collaboration between men and women.

A good guideline for all you do is the golden rule. Be honest. Be ethical. Don't steal from the company. Don't steal for the company. Do an honest day's work, and turn out a quality product. You may not make as much money as you otherwise might, but why make the world a worse place? Both good and bad behavior are contagious. In a recent business recession, an insurance man told me that his clients were sticking with him, and that it was less for economic reasons than because of the way he had always treated them.

Think of your work as somehow building the reign of God in the world. That is the Christian way of looking at it, a falling in behind Jesus in continuation of what he was trying to do in the world—to make it a better place in accordance with God's vision for it. Every work contributes something to the maintenance or development of cosmic life. All you have to do is imagine the world without the effort of some humble contributor—the man who sweeps the streets, the woman on the manufacturer's assembly line, the kid who serves you your fast food—and you will see what a difference each person's work makes. Everybody benefits from your doing a quality job.

Work to make the system just—your company, your industry, your profession. Don't exploit foreign labor. Keep the profit margin reasonable. Think globally. Work locally. You may have more impact than you know in widening concentric circles.

Work with an ecological perspective. Prevent harm to the air, the land, the water, the wildlife. Work for a just distribution of goods, not just in our country but throughout the world. Recent developments have made it clear that we are compelled to establish a mutually enhancing human presence on the planet, or the whole interdependent system (organism) perishes. In the words of ethicist Daniel Maguire, "If present trends continue, we won't." So our perspective has to widen from the profit-motive alone to concern for a healthy planet.

Spirituality is not a separate activity, but a dimension of everything we do. There are many opportunities to heighten this dimension in the work place.

Reading Suggestions

Richard Bolles, *What Color Is Your Parachute?* (Berkeley, CA: Ten Speed Press, 1987), is a helpful workbook for those trying to find their niche in the work world.

Mark Bryan, Julia Cameron, Catherine Allen, *The Artist's Way at Work: Twelve Ways to Creative Freedom* (New York: William Morrow and Company, 1998), is a workbook for finding your own voice at work, as well as in the rest of your life.

William Cleary, ed., *Selving: Linking Work to Spirituality* (Milwaukee, WI: Marquette University Press, 2000), offers a fine collection of essays bringing spiritual perspectives to the work place.

Gregory Pierce, *Spirituality at Work: Ten Ways to Balance Your Life on the Job* (Chicago: Loyola University Press, 2001), is filled with practical ideas for spiritualizing your work, some of which are incorporated here. The author invites responses and keeps the dialogue going at gfapierce@aol.com.

Thomas Berry is one of the leading proponents of an ecological vision. See his *The Dream of the Earth* (San Francisco: Sierra Club Books, 1988), or Thomas Berry with Thomas Clarke, *A Theology of Reconciliation between Humans and the Earth* (Mystic, CT: Twenty-third Publications, 1991).

10

UNDERSTANDING HOMOPHOBIA

Have you ever noticed, when the topic of homosexuality comes up, the sheer strength of many people's antihomosexual feelings? Have you wondered where all this emotion is coming from? What gay people may do in their lives really concerns most people very little, if you think about it, yet they have this vehement passion to stamp it, or them, out. What is this? And what is it that prompts a group of young men, at a loss for what to do on a Friday night, to say, "Let's go out and pound up a couple of fags?"

Prejudice is a fixed and closed negative state of mind—literally "a judgment made in advance." One of the things I have learned about common prejudices is that they are rooted in ignorance and fear. The fear flows from the ignorance. We instinctively fear the unknown, because we cannot size it up and figure out how to deal with it. So if we want to loosen the grip of homophobia on us, we would have to go to its roots, replacing ignorance with knowledge, and ascertaining how substantive our fears really are.

Facing Our Ignorance

Straight people often believe that gay people *choose* their same-sex orientation. That is the first and largest piece of ignorance. Just think a minute. Who would choose it? It is ostracism and a life of suffering. It is living with prejudice, expressions of hatred, and antigay jokes. It is being told that you are a pervert, mentally ill, abominable in the eyes of God. It is being denied the job that you would like or the home you wish to buy or rent. It means never being able to marry and have a family, not only joys in themselves, but a ticket to social respectability. It means facing the difficult choice, again and again, between being closeted and being out. If you choose the closet, you live a double life, carry a dark secret in every social situation, and are always in danger of being found out—which might mean the loss of your family, friends, job, or reputation. If you choose coming out, you run all these same risks instantly, and when you walk the street you are in danger of being assaulted. I ask again: Who would *choose* to be gay?

Here is a bit of personal testimony on this point from a man willing to tell his story.

> I didn't want to be homosexual. I hadn't chosen homosexuality as a "lifestyle." In fact, I spent the next three and a half decades trying to overcome my "sickness" and to seek God's forgiveness for my sin. I read the bible and prayed frantically. I married and had children. I confessed my struggle to my young bride and for twenty-three years we spent more than $100,000 on Christian therapy to help me get over being homosexual. I didn't act on my homosexual feelings....I practiced meditation, biofeedback, and daily spiritual discipline. I underwent electric-shock therapy. I was even exorcised. Finally, desperate and depressed, I slashed my wrists and hoped to die. At that point, Lyla, my wonderful wife, intervened. "I like gay people," she said. "I just didn't want you to be one. But you are and I have to accept that. You've been a good husband and father. Now I want you to be free to experience life as

> an equally good gay man." We both wept as I packed my suitcase and moved from our family home.

There are other areas of ignorance. If it is learned that someone is gay, immediately all aspects of that person's being and life are called into question. They are queers, weirdos, people entirely different from the rest of us. But this is not the case either. Our sexual orientation is just one dimension of us. There is a lot more to any person than his or her sexuality. Think of your parents, for instance, or your close friends—or yourself. How big a factor, in the total picture of these lives, is the individual's sexuality? That, incidentally, is the trouble with calling a person *a homosexual.* This is a label, and it suggests that now we know everything we need to know about this person, whereas we know *next to nothing* about him or her. How much do I know about you if I learn that you are *a heterosexual?* What is *a heterosexual?* What is *a homosexual?* That is why it is better not to use nouns, but adjectives here and in similar cases. And the adjectives *gay* (which is used for both men and women) and *lesbian* are preferable to the clinical term *homosexual,* because most of us would prefer not to have clinical terms applied to us in social life—even if we have a few coming.

Another thing straight people tend to assume about gay people is that they are dangerous. Those who run campaigns to deny gay people ordinary civil rights typically claim, "If we allow them to teach in our schools, they will teach this to our children! And they will sexually abuse our children!" You can imagine the fear that stirs up.

You can safely assume that gay people are just like straight people in all respects, the only difference being that their sexual attraction is to the same rather than the opposite sex. Gay men do abuse children sometimes, but no study has ever shown that they do this more than straight men do. The gay population is estimated at 10 percent or more of the total population, yet

95 percent of reported pedophilia cases are of little girls being abused by older males. But most straight men are not pedophiles. Neither are most gay men. In tests of mental health, gay persons consistently show full equality with their straight peers, which is remarkable when you consider how much rejection, often abetted by self-hate, they have suffered.

What would it mean for gay people to "teach this to our children"? We are not taught our sexual orientation; we find ourselves with it. If sexual orientation were taught by modeling, how can the presence of gay children in straight homes, an environment much more formative than school, be explained? But that is exactly where gay people come from and in large numbers. When I ask my gay clients who as young adults married and had children (because at the time it seemed the only thing to do), what their adult children are doing now, I learn that most of them are married and have families. So their children are not gay. I remember a gay client who was one of five sons in his family, and he was the only one who was gay. How did that happen? The best part of his story was that his family warmly accepted him, in the same spirit that they accepted all the rest of the variety among them.

Well, do gay men hate women? Do lesbian women hate men? A few do—probably in about the same proportions as straight men hate women, and straight women hate men. This is another stereotype. Do men and women typically hate the gender to which they are not sexually attracted? No, the issue is not love and hate, but only sexual orientation.

One final area of ignorance. Religious people in significant numbers believe that the Bible condemns homosexuality. Even irreligious homophobic people like to mention this, because it gives them such a respectable cloak for their prejudice. But it is by no means clear that the Bible condemns homosexuality. Many scholars are quite convinced, on careful examination of the very few biblical texts that speak of homosexuality at all, that the Bible does not give us any basis for an across-the-board condemnation of homosexuality. The biblical writers were not asking today's questions about homosexuality, and so they were not answering them either. To take a single example, if you read what St. Paul has to say about homosexuality in Romans (1:18–32), it is clear that he misunderstands it. He thinks that the homosexual person is really a heterosexual who has freely and perversely set that aside in favor of homosexual relating. He also thinks that the reason people do this is that they have abandoned God, and so God has abandoned them. Our contemporary experience profoundly challenges both ideas. Gay men and women wish they could be straight, and many are people of deep faith. On the basis of the way scholars now read biblical texts critically in their historical context, we see a growing movement in both church and synagogue to bless same-sex marriages and to ordain openly gay clergy. There is no way that this could be happening if the Bible clearly condemned all same-sex partnerships as sinful.

My first field is theology, my second psychology. One thing that has become abundantly clear to me in listening to the religious discussion of homosexuality through the years is that the prejudice comes first, then the theology, not the other way around. If you have the antihomosexual bias, the theological argument serves you well. Racists too have long appealed to biblical texts to justify their bigotry. Slave-owners find biblical texts to justify slavery, and sexists find biblical texts to justify sexism. But if you do not have an antihomosexual bias, it will strike you at once, when you see it spelled out, how weak the theological case against homosexuality is.

A final item of ignorance is that AIDS is a gay disease, from which it follows that if we allow homosexuality we are furthering the spread of AIDS. Ironically, the fact that AIDS was at first regarded as a disease restricted to homosexual persons and drug addicts was precisely the reason the Reagan Administration allocated so little money for AIDS research when the disease first appeared in the United States. What loss to anyone if people of this sort died out?

But a recent U.N. report sets the real facts before us. AIDS is not a homosexual disease, but a sexually transmitted disease. Most persons in the world with HIV/AIDS are heterosexual. As many women have died of AIDS as men. Sub-Saharan Africa has 70 percent of the world's 33.6 million HIV/AIDS cases today. There, women make up more than 50 percent of the infected. Forty million African children are already orphans to AIDS. Asia, with 60 percent of the world's population and the steepest infection curve, is soon to become the epicenter of this disaster. Unless something is done quickly, more people will die of AIDS in the first decade of the twenty-first century than died in all the wars of the twentieth century. That is why the United Nations has mounted an urgent campaign to press for the necessary research, education, and treatment, all quite haphazardly pursued so far.

Naming Our Fears

Sometimes ignorance leads the way in generating our prejudices, sometimes fear. What are some common fears regarding gay people?

Immediately, you might protest: "I do not fear gay men. In fact, I feel utter contempt for them. They are weaklings, women. I could pound one up in a minute." But why would you pound one up? Do you pound women up too? And is personal superiority proved by physical dominance? Then our top boxers and wrestlers are our most estimable countrymen. But whence the need to establish superiority in the first place?

Psychiatrist Carl Jung pointed out that when we find ourselves hating someone, we will probably also find that what we hate in that person is a quality we hate in ourselves. We hate and kill outside ourselves what we cannot accept inside ourselves. In the present case, that is our "feminine" part. Our boyhood conditioning taught us that anything smacking of the "feminine" in ourselves was something of which to be ashamed. So now as "real men" we pride ourselves on having entirely obliterated all that. Actually, we have not. It still lives in us, though feebly. That it badly needs development, so that we can be whole human beings, is the thesis of this book. But if we continue to believe the message we received as boys, we will keep trying instead to eradicate the last vestige of "femininity" in ourselves, lest we lose some supposed superiority to women and gay men.

There are other fears as well. How do you talk to a gay man? He's just plain weird, right? Actually, you have been talking to gay men all your life, without realizing that they were gay. You respect and like many of them, their gayness being hidden from you. So you already know how to talk to gay men—the same way you talk to straight men, and to women. There is a rich variety among us all, but the broad base of our common humanity stands firm and always serves for connection.

But won't a gay man come on to me? Probably not, any more than a straight man comes on to every woman he sees. But he might, and if he did it would give you some insight into the experience of women, regarded first as sex objects by quite a few straight men. If a gay man does come on to you, all you have to say is no thanks. No need to become indignant or to reject the man. He cannot help his sexual orientation or interest any more than you can help yours, and there is certainly no reason to run from him. If he finds you attractive, it will be for the same reasons that some women find you attractive. It would be a gross misunderstanding, yet common enough, to think his attraction to you means that *you* are gay. There was a very sad incident a few years ago when a male television personality was surprised to learn that the fan who wanted to meet him on a talk show was gay and had a crush on him. When he learned this, he killed the man—to clear his good name. What a tragedy. His good name was never in question.

Is there any truth to the rumor that gay men and lesbian women are a threat to the family? This is often enough proclaimed, but has anyone ever explained how? I have never found them a threat to my family. What can they do to it? Do they somehow hurt it by expanding the notion of family by their own partnerships? That still does not hurt my family or any family I know. I suppose you could say that they have hurt the families they created when they went against their sexual orientation and got married, then had children, only to face the truth about themselves later and leave those families. But if we stop trying to force people into boxes that they do not fit in, gay persons will most likely stop attempting to make straight marriage work for them.

Gay men have the reputation of being sexually promiscuous. They often are. But are they any more promiscuous than straight men? And would not many straight men be much more promiscuous if they could just get women to go along with their desires? But here they run into women's general disinclination to enter into sex without love. Gay men have an easier time of it. They can get the sex they want from other gay men, often without the love question being asked. Might some of the hatred straight men feel against gay men be envy over this ready availability of sex?

Straight men sometimes hate lesbian women as much as they hate gay men. Why? Do they take it personally and feel insulted that a woman could prefer another woman to themselves? Or that two women make it quite well through life without the help of a man? Do they feel affronted because they presume that lesbian women hate men? But, again, what sort of logic concludes that if women are not sexually attracted to men it means they hate them? Or is all this simply ignorance breeding fear—I haven't got the slightest idea what sort of human this is, and I'm out of here. Again, it is only her sexual orientation that is different. How big a factor is that in the total picture of her life?

Often an element of sheer distaste figures into the rejection of homosexuality. We feel no attraction to the sort of sexual expression in which gay people engage; in fact, it may repel us. No problem. No one is asking us to engage in those behaviors. Can we show equal respect for the freedom of others? And how, when we consider what a wonderful part of life sex is, can we find it in our hearts to tell gay persons that it is somehow their destiny to live their lives without it?

Gay men do challenge straight men's notions of what it means to be male. Here we come, I believe, to the heart of the problem. This is very uncomfortable and generates a lot of anxiety. It hits at the heart of the macho mystique. It destroys the possibility of a black and white reality. A gay man, with his so-called feminine traits, makes a straight man recognize some of the great gaps in his own personal development—his feeling life, his compassion and gentleness, his artistic side, his spiritual life, his aesthetic capacity, in short, his inner life. In many ways, it is easier to exterminate gay men from the face of the earth than to face and acknowledge this valid critique.

The fact is, each of us has a measure of same-sex attraction in us, and a measure of opposite-sex attraction, a measure of "feminine" traits and a measure of "masculine" traits. We all lie at some point on a broad spectrum, with hypothetically pure types at both ends, and the rest of us, each with a unique blend of traits and attractions, in the wide space between them. If we could ever learn to acknowledge and love *all* the parts of ourselves (perhaps it is a grace), we would stop hating people who more clearly embody dimensions of our being that we have denied or failed to develop.

Getting Free of Prejudice

Clearing up misunderstandings and discovering that our fears are baseless carries us a long ways toward the dissolving of prejudice. But if we would eliminate it entirely, we have to have face-to-face contact and dialogue with those persons we have misunderstood and feared. Let me share a personal story.

I became aware of my sexual curiosity and attractions early. They were straight and they were strong. I went to Catholic schools, and we were taught that anything the least bit sexual was sinful (except in marriage, which was a long ways off). I paid no particular attention to the few mentions of homosexuality made in our catechesis. It was not my issue. And I did not know anyone gay. Matters might still lie thus today, except for an incident some six years into seminary life.

There, when I was about twenty-four, a good friend of mine told me one day that he was gay. He told me precisely because we were good friends, and he was just then really struggling over what he was becoming more and more aware of. It was a very asexual environment we lived in. My friend was not sexually active. I don't think any of us were at that time. But Jack was becoming aware of same-sex attractions, and he did not like them. He hated them, in fact, but there they were.

What struck me more than anything was the pain he was in. He felt "different," and in his differentness terribly alone. He wondered if his discovery meant that he should leave the seminary. He sought guidance on that from those more experienced than I was. What he laid before me was his keen inner suffering. It moved me, because I cared about him.

It is possible that if Jack had entered the seminary saying, "I am gay," I might never have paid any attention to him. What did he have to do with me? I might even have thought him dangerous. But sexuality was rarely discussed among us in those days. I met Jack as a person, and found him a beautiful man—warm, deep, spiritual, sensitive, with a fine mind and a great sense of humor. I used to love taking walks with him. We talked about so many things. The whole point is this: First I knew the person, and I loved him; then I learned that he was gay. That challenged my worldview. A person of this extraordinary quality could be gay! Besides that, it was clear that he did not want to be gay at all. He longed for nothing so much as to be able to rip it out and cast it away. But there it was, undeniable, irremovable. He had to come to acceptance, then figure out how to live with it. All of this was new to me, easily one of the more valuable illuminations of my young life.

Jack did decide to leave the seminary, and we bade each other a sad farewell. Unfortunately, I have lost track of him. But I will always remember him as a wonderful friend, and I am still grateful for the enlightenment that he gave me.

It would be another fifteen years before I would leave the Jesuits myself, for the simple reason that I wanted to marry. Now I am a therapist and continue to be a spiritual guide. I have met several hundred more Jacks—and Jills—through the years, and listened with compassion and respect to their stories. The fundamental features are the same: good person, unhappy discovery, vigorous attempts to have it otherwise, much inner suffering, and hard questions about whom to share the news with and how to live one's life. Of the hundreds, maybe thousands, of gay men and women I have come to know, I can think of only three or four men and one woman I didn't like. And there has been only one gay man who has come on to me sexually. I told him, even as we shared a warm hug, which is what turned him on, that I could not meet him there. It is thirty years later now, and he and I are still close friends. "At first I was in love with you," he said. "I had to work it through. Now I just love you."

Today I grieve over the oppression of gay people by society and church. It is so wrongheaded, destructive, and wasteful. Life is hard enough for everybody without adding oppression to it. Being gay is challenge enough in itself without the hatred, contempt, and violence of straight people heaped on top of it. This proud, passionate rejection is rooted in ignorance and fear. Who has the problem? Who needs to change? Not gay people, but homophobic straight people. Again, we are talking about spirituality here—about a change of heart, justice, and love.

How do we overcome our homophobia? We have to come to know gay people as persons and listen to them as they tell their stories. That is all. If we wish to overcome our anti-Jewish or antiblack prejudice, the approach is exactly the same. And we have just about as far to seek to find a gay person to learn from as we would a black or Jewish person. They are all around us—among our fellow students, fellow workers, neighbors, friends, and extended family. They simply have not told us.

Reading Suggestions

The story of the Reagan Administration's indifference to the growing AIDS crisis is poignantly told by San Francisco journalist Randy Shilts in his *And the Band Played On: Politics, People, and the AIDS Epidemic* (New York: St. Martin's Press, 1987; reissued in paperback by same press in 2000).

The AIDS situation around the world at the present time is documented in the *Joint United Nations Programme on HIV/AIDS (UNAIDS), Report on the Global HIV/AIDS Epidemic* (Geneva, Switzerland: UNAIDS, 2000).

Patricia Jung and Ralph Smith, *Heterosexism: An Ethical Challenge* (Albany, NY: State University of New York Press, 1993), offer a scholarly critique of biblical and philosophical arguments against same-sex relations, challenging the churches to a deeper examination.

Other books reflecting critically on the theological case against homosexual relations are John Boswell, *Christianity, Social Tolerance, and Homosexuality* (Chicago: University of Chicago Press, 1980); John McNeill, *The Church and the Homosexual* (Boston: Beacon Press, 1988); James B. Nelson,

Embodiment: An Approach to Sexuality and Christian Theology (Cleveland: Pilgrim Press, 1980), and *Between Two Gardens: Reflections on Sexuality and Religious Experience* (Cleveland: Pilgrim Press, 1983).

The personal story of the man who tried to find a cure for his homosexuality is that of Mel White as told in "Courage: To Thine Own Self" in Sarah Ban Breathnach and friends, Michael Segell, ed., *A Man's Journey to Simple Abundance* (New York: Scribner, 2000), 198.

John McNeill, *Taking a Chance on God: Liberating Theology for Gays, Lesbians, and Their Lovers, Families, and Friends* (Boston: Beacon Press, 1988), speaks a spiritual message of comfort from the perspective of Christian faith.

11

RIGHTING THE BALANCE WITH WOMEN

Male privilege and power are deeply entrenched in our social system. This fact is obvious to women, but evident to only some men. That is because those who are benefiting from a system very rarely recognize the inequities of the system. You feel those only from the lower rungs on the ladder, or from the outside looking in. Male privilege and power constitute a serious problem. It is a problem because it is inherently unfair. It also causes much suffering and stands in the way of much good.

The inherent injustice of the gender system can be made more conspicuous if we turn it on its head. Suppose that at a wedding, the mother of the groom brought him up the aisle and turned him over to his bride—two women exchanging a man. Suppose that after a couple took their vows in a wedding ceremony, the officiating minister said: "I pronounce you woman and husband." Suppose that those who wrote the Bible were women instead of men, and so, in recounting the creation, instead of saying, "Male and female created He them," said, "Female and male created She them." That would be a fundamentally different map of reality from the very top, wouldn't it? Suppose that then women, naturally in charge of all the churches, taught that in a family the woman is breadwinner, and the man homemaker, according to a complementarity built into nature by God. What if in a polygamous society, a woman were allowed to have many husbands but a man could only have one wife? What if in a monogamous society, it were pretty much taken for granted that women would fool around sexually but men would not? Suppose that in the business world, nearly all the CEOs were women, and nearly all their secretaries men. Suppose that at family gatherings on Thanksgiving and Christmas, the women watched television while the men served them the drinks and dinner that they had prepared and then did the cleanup.

I am not promoting such a society. It is just the same oppression reversed. I sketch it only so that the contours of the present system might become more clearly visible.

Let me now present another vision, a dream I do consider worth striving for. Fantasize half the podiums and half the pulpits of the world occupied by women. Imagine that half the Supreme Court justices, half of all the judges in the land, and half the governors and mayors were women. Suppose that half the representatives in all the world's congresses were women, and half the faculties of its universities, as well as half its bishops, and half the time its pope—though we would have to shelve the word pope during those periods because it means *papa,* and *mama* would be in charge. Suppose that at weddings nobody gave anybody away, but the bride and groom walked down the aisle together like the two mature individuals they supposedly are, and turned and welcomed their guests. Suppose that in families, men and women shared the responsibilities of breadwinning and homemaking equally, that their covenants with one another were monogamous on both sides, and that at family celebrations they waited on each other in equal measure. Suppose that God were referred to sometimes as he, sometimes as she, sometimes as neither, because human gender categories hardly apply to the Mystery.

No question that what we are contemplating here is nothing less than the overhaul of the social system and the fashioning of a brave new world. Would the new society be any better than the old? Hard to say. But what would we have to lose by trying it? Look at the world we are living in now. Men have been in charge of it for a long, long time. And it is filled with inequity, conflict, and anguish.

Those who have power are usually very reluctant to give it up. Must we have a bloody revolution, in which the oppressed in vast numbers rise up and wrest power from those who hold it? Or dare we dream of a revolutionary *free act*—a *peaceful* redistribution of power flowing from a spiritual awakening? Might we live to see men, recognizing the gross injustice of the present system, the suffering that it causes, the contributions that it deprives us of, freely give back to women the power they have taken from them? Could men recognize and acknowledge the equality of women and invite them into fully collaborative relationship? That would be nothing less than the realization of Jesus' driving passion—the coming of the reign of God into the world—in at least one momentous respect.

What Do Women Want?

From my counseling experience with men and women, individually and in couples, and from my reading of the literature of the women's movement, here is how I would summarize what women want from men. Not that women have it all together and the work to be done lies solely on the male side. Women have their own failings, struggles, and growth challenges. But here our focus is on male growth, and women have some helpful feedback for us. There are five main areas of concern.

1. *That we be nonviolent.* In a recent survey in which men were asked what they most feared from women, and women what they most feared from men, the men answered: being laughed at by women. The women answered: being raped or murdered by men. There isn't much proportionality here, is there? Men laugh at women too, and that is probably no less

painful to women than to men. But to women, that seems a pretty trifling thing compared to what they are really up against. It is estimated that about 25 percent of girls and women have been sexually abused by a male. Domestic violence is widespread, far more common than most of us are aware of, and it cuts across all classes. The threat of it is ever a possibility even where it has not yet occurred. A woman dare not walk down the street at night and had better be alert when she walks by day. This is the real world for women, and it is always charged with the threat of physical violence.

In Montreal in 1989, a 25-year-old man denounced "feminists" and shot fourteen women dead in a rampage at the École Polytechnique. The carnage prompted three men to step forward and start a campaign against violence against women. Here are some excerpts from their "White Ribbon" statement:

> If it were between countries, we'd call it a war.... But it's happening to women, and it's just an everyday affair. It is violence against women. It is rape at home and on dates. It is the beating or the blow that one out of four Canadian women receive in their lifetime. It is the sexual harassment at work and sexual abuse of the young. It is murder.
>
> There's no secret enemy pulling the trigger. No unseen virus that leads to death. It's just men. Men from all social backgrounds and of all colors and ages. Men in business suits and men in blue collars.... Just regular guys.
>
> All those regular guys, though, have helped create a climate of fear and mistrust among women. Our sisters and our mothers, our daughters and our lovers can no longer feel safe in their homes. At night they can't walk to the corner for milk without wondering who's walking

> behind them....Even the millions of women in relationships with that majority of men who are gentle and caring, feel they cannot totally trust men. All women are imprisoned in a culture of violence.
>
> Men have been defined as part of the problem. But we are writing this statement because we think men can also be part of the solution. Confronting men's violence requires nothing less than a commitment to full equality for women and a redefinition of what it means to be men, to discover a meaning to manhood that doesn't require blood to be spilled.

2. *That we respect women as equals.* So simple a request, but what a challenging idea to many men. We are often taught, or somehow assume, that we are better than women, more important, and meant to be in charge. What nerve when a woman calls that into question, does not instinctively sense her proper place, and fails to be amiable and supportive from the periphery. But if you ask what is the basis of this conviction of superiority, it is very hard to find an answer that will stand scrutiny.

The only clear area of male superiority is physical strength. Surely that is quite low on the ladder of human possibilities. Can men claim that they are more intelligent, more spiritual, more artistic, deeper and more complex, better at organization, superior in human relations, or just plain more gifted cumulatively than women are? As soon as you put it into words, it is plain that men could never establish this. How is it, then, that men have all the power, that men run the world? Does it come down finally to that superior physical strength? If that is the case, we have just stumbled upon a huge and embarrassing discovery. For then it is by violence and the threat of violence that men have laid down the law and kept women in a subordinate position, starting with the family, and moving out to ever-wider circles of power. Wow! It just may not be so conspicuous anymore, because whole systems are so in place and subtly legitimated by cultural conditioning that the hard fist of man need not so often appear. A display of anger now and then along with glass ceilings and glass doors suffice to preserve what has been established.

This, then, is a crucial question for us as men, and it is a soul question. Do we respect woman as equals? If we say yes, do we live that out in practice?

How would we know? There would be signs. We would listen respectfully and let ourselves be influenced. We would not find it strange that a woman be in authority over us, or that our wife might make more money than we do or be better educated. We would support our daughters' life-ambitions as much as our sons'. We would not expect personal service from women, but would offer it to them in equal or greater measure. We would not sexually harass women any more than we want to be sexually harassed. We would support women's efforts to liberate themselves from all the oppressions so long in place. We would even express our repentance for how we have contributed to that, or at least failed to oppose it, because our male-centeredness has profoundly hurt our mothers, sisters, daughters, wives, and friends.

3. *That we let ourselves feel and share our feelings.* So important is this that we have devoted a separate chapter to it. This is the area in which men generally most need to grow just to be fully human. Without it, we are one-dimensional, boring, and dangerous.

4. *That we be empathetic.* Empathy, a crucial sector of our world of feeling, is the capacity to enter into the feelings of another. It starts with a careful listening, and then imagining what that person's experience might be like. If we listen to

women, we will learn what it is like to live inside a woman's body—what it feels like to have a monthly period, to carry and deliver a baby, to go through menopause. We will learn what it feels like to offer a suggestion at a meeting and have no attention paid to it—until a man proposes the very same idea. We will learn what it feels like to be physically smaller and weaker in a world full of stronger humans, and what happens inside you when your mate, who is at least twice as strong as you, takes hold of you and shakes you. We might also learn what it feels like to be reduced to a sex object. Feeling is the basis of caring. When we succeed in getting inside women's experience, we become part of the solution instead of just another part of the problem.

5. *That we be coparents and cultivate a close relationship with each of our children.* This topic too is so important that we have devoted a separate chapter to it. At the core of the matter is the way we conceive of our role with respect to our children. Is parenting women's work? Are we just providers and enforcers, or are we coresponsible?

You will know you have achieved coresponsibility when you find yourself thinking as much about each of your kids' needs as you do about the challenges of your job. Your kids will bring you their pains and struggles as readily as they bring them to their mother. And you will look forward to getting home at night not so much to have a drink, read the paper, and watch the game, as to spend time with your wife and kids.

If you think about it, what women are asking is indeed a stretch for men, but it is not unreasonable. And wouldn't it make our lives richer and more satisfying? Contrast this vision with "The Ten Commandments of Patriarchy," as drafted by a man who has worked extensively with men's groups. Patriarchy is that male-devised social system in which men rule the world, and these "Commandments" are the rules by which they live.

1. Thou shalt not cry or expose any feeling or emotion, especially fear, weakness, or empathy.
2. Thou shalt not be vulnerable, but logical, rational, and strong.
3. Thou shalt have no other egos before thee.
4. Thou shalt have an answer to every problem, and be in command of every crisis.
5. Thou shalt be condescending to women in all ways big and small.
6. Thou shalt control thy wife's body and relationships.
7. Thou shalt have no breadwinners before thee.
8. Thou shalt not be responsible for housework before anybody.
9. Thou shalt not listen, except to find fault.
10. Thou shalt never participate in any form of introspection.

The Failure of the "Men's Movement"

The problem with the "men's movement" as it has developed so far is not only that it has failed to reach most men, but that it has not pursued the really important goals. It has not laid out the core problems wrought by sexism, nor has it challenged men to radical change.

Part of the movement has clustered around Robert Bly and his book *Iron John.* Bly has called men into the forest to regroup, beat drums, and fortify traditional notions of masculinity. He rejects the "male bashing" coming from the women's movement, finds some men today too soft, and tries to help men generally feel better about themselves the way they are more accustomed to being. Needless to say, his is a very different vision from mine.

But we can be grateful to Robert Bly for two very helpful ideas. The first is that the key to a man's finding his world of feeling is his grieving his relationship with his father—what might have been and never was. Many men carry the wound of being neglected by their fathers. Some were physically or verbally abused. Bly has helped many get in touch with that and grieve it together in men's groups. His second helpful insight is that young men need male mentors in the work place, to introduce them into that world and help them be their best there. Typically, there is little or no help offered, and the young man has to find his way alone. Bly's mentoring idea would bring great enrichment to this important sector of a man's development.

In the other main branch of the men's movement, Promise Keepers, which originated in the religious quarter, the main message is that men should take charge of the spiritual lives of their families. While the area of spirituality is clearly one in which men need to grow, Promise Keepers never calls the social system itself into question, with its presumption that the male is properly head of the house and therefore should also be in charge of the spiritual life of the family. The spirituality espoused by Promise Keepers also lacks the comprehensiveness it needs to call men to a complete change of heart in their relationships with women, children, and the world at large.

Undoubtedly, some in the religious sector would point out in defense of the Promise Keepers' approach, that in the Bible the man is head of the household, and that in a classic passage in the New Testament on marriage the man is called the head of his wife (Eph 5:24). This is true, but the Bible in this respect is part of the problem, not of the solution. Its writers were all men, writing from within a patriarchal culture. Even the authors of sacred texts tend to take their cultural presuppositions for granted. That is why the Bible has long been a rich resource for buttressing many of our favorite prejudices: racism, homophobia, sexism, slavery, polygamy, capital punishment, and war.

In sum, neither branch of the men's movement speaks to the real problem, nor asks very much of men. And now both seem to be fading out.

The religions have generally accepted and even supported the oppression of women. Recognizing this, an international group of male scholars, each an expert on his own religion, recently undertook an important research project. They asked themselves this question: Are there any resources within our religious traditions, especially in our sacred writings, for redressing this situation of injustice? And their research delivered a resounding yes, from each of the traditions—Buddhist, Hindu, Jewish, Christian, Muslim, Native American, Native African. These scholars found that there are broad principles of justice, even specifically of gender justice, in the sacred writings of each tradition. These basic principles, they assert, must take precedence over more particular laws that were developed by male leaders in the later evolution of each community's life. Cognizant of the power of religion in the shaping of culture, these men have added the weight of their findings to women's struggle for justice, insisting that religion can be authentic only if it puts its energies into righting the long-standing wrong of women's oppression.

All of us are familiar with the story of Beauty and the Beast. Beauty is beautiful, of course; the beast is shaggy and ugly, even frightening. The beast is smitten with Beauty and asks her for her love. Beauty refuses, many times over. But one day, in a moment of compassion, she kisses the beast, and he is transformed into a handsome prince.

This is a charming story of transformation under love's influence. But are we men transformed by a woman's kiss or even by her love over time? Not necessarily. We can slouch right on as the same shaggy beasts with women's kisses upon us. It takes a free choice and a certain dedication to become a handsome prince. The change has to come mainly from our side. And why should we have to be kissed by a woman to get started? Why not show up at the table as a handsome prince and take Beauty's breath away?

Reading Suggestions

For "The Ten Commandments of Patriarchy," I am indebted to Frederick Grosse, *The Eight Masks of Men* (New York: Haworth Press, 1998). I have edited them slightly.

Robert Bly, *Iron John* (Reading, MA: Addison-Wesley, 1990), played a key role in launching the men's movement.

For a thorough evaluation of Promise Keepers from different perspectives, see Dane S. Claussen, ed., *Standing on the Promises: The Promise Keepers and the Revival of Manhood* (Cleveland: Pilgrim Press, 1999).

Kay Leigh Hagan, ed., *Women Respond to the Men's Movement* (HarperSanFrancisco, 1992), is a fine collection of short pieces by women, not only critiquing the men's movement but expressing their own principal justice concerns. The Canadian White Ribbon statement is from page 166 of this book.

The group that did the research on the religions is called The Religious Consultation on Population, Reproductive Health, and Ethics. Their research is published in John C. Raines and Daniel C. Maguire, eds., *What Men Owe to Women: Men's Voices from World Religions* (Albany: State University of New York Press, 2001). Summing up, Roman Catholic ethicist and coeditor of the research, Daniel Maguire, offers a perspective on why these scholars got involved:

> We see religion as a positive response to the sacred that issues into advocacy and commitment....We see religion as an appreciative, enhancing response to the preciousness of life, a preciousness that merits our supreme

linguistic encomium *sacred*....Realistic social analysis should recognize that two-thirds of the world's people affiliate with some religion and the other third is affected by the gravitational pull generated by these symbol-filled cultural powerhouses....Our common assumption in the Consultation "school" is that the religions we study all have elements of a rich sense of justice that becomes our normative rubric for assessing, embracing, or dismissing ideas and practices that have arisen in the traditions....In all of our projects, the *empowerment of women* is seen as the key to progress on every one of our issues. (pp. 282–83)

12

LIVING YOUR LIFE SPIRITUALLY

This whole book has been about male spirituality, but that may need a clearer elaboration. The book has repeatedly called men to a change of heart and a whole new way of living. That is what authentic spirituality is all about. It has been an exhortation to men to cultivate the best qualities of the human spirit and to reach the fullness of their possibilities as human persons. But that is spirituality's whole point: that we become good human beings and live out our destiny.

Charting a Spiritual Course

Let us revisit the book's main themes, drawing out their spiritual dimension more explicitly. The exhortation to let yourself feel and to share the feelings you have, including your weakness and fear and inadequacy, is a call to authenticity, and so into spiritual living. It means the end of posturing, the voluntary surrender of your mask, the embracing of your humanity whole, and a humbler, gentler presentation of yourself to the world. The exhortation to integrate your sexual energy into responsible loving, so that it is not a destructive force hurting other people but an ingredient in appropriate expressions of love, is a call to a spiritualized way of living. You are no longer seeking just your own gratification, but authentic and responsible relationship. The same applies to mastering your anger and violence. It involves recognizing the harm that they can do to others, and bringing them under control out of reverence for others.

Relating to your spouse as a fully equal partner, consistently showing concern for her well-being and fulfillment, is how you live a spiritual life in marriage. It means dedicating yourself to true love with all that that entails. The same is true of real parenting, which demands being a generously loving man, fully engaged in the lives of your children.

Finding your true self is a matter of becoming and being that person you were made to be, so it is living your destiny before God. Making efforts to practice justice and love in your work place is clearly a spiritual choice. Overcoming prejudice of any kind, homophobia or any other hurtful bias, is a matter both of justice and of truth. It means renouncing hatred, exclusion, and violence, and replacing them with acceptance, love, and respect. That is a journey of the soul. Giving back to women half the power we have seized or had handed to us by our forebears requires a renunciation of what is unjustly held, and adherence to a new sense of fairness. This involves several virtues—honesty, humility, contrition, justice. Collaborating with women and men of goodwill everywhere to create a world in which all people, not just the privileged, can enjoy fullness of life, and all nonhuman beings can also thrive, is a dedication that can only be called spiritual. All of this requires self-transcendence, a breaking open of one's egocentric vision and horizons. That is the hallmark of spirituality, which is always a movement into harmony with the larger energies of the universe.

Spirituality and Religion

Is this a complete picture of spirituality? Is it simply seeking to do what is right, deliberately cultivating virtues like justice and love? Or is it more complicated than that? What is religion, and how does religion relate to spirituality?

The virtuous life is the *goal* of religion. Religion does not always succeed in producing it, but this is what it is for. The virtuous life and the spiritual life are one and the same and are the highest expression of the human spirit. The role of religion is to support and nurture this kind of spiritual living.

Spirituality is prior to religion. It is religion's root. Our relationship with Mystery is a given in life, or at least it is a constant offer. Spirit is the wind all around us, the breath we breathe in and out. Since the Mystery is present to us always, we need not go to church or synagogue to find it or even to cultivate our relationship with it. The Spirit is always already alive within us. It keeps us hopeful amid the trials of life and quietly draws us toward doing good. Put most simply, spirituality is our lived relationship with Mystery.

But the experience of the Spirit or the Mystery, particularly when it is intense, moves people to create religion. Spiritual experience and spiritual longing organize themselves into the structures of religion, and religion goes on to support and nourish the life of the Spirit. A religion typically develops creed, code, and cult. Creed is the set of beliefs about the Mystery and its relationship to us. Code is the set of rules by which we are to live in relationship with the Mystery. Cult is the ritual in which we worship the Mystery and draw its power into our lives. Gradually, buildings are built for religious communities, leadership is organized, and religion becomes the matrix within which the spiritual life is lived.

Who Needs Religion? Or Spirituality?

Organized religion is much criticized today. In the West, people are leaving the mainline Christian churches in significant numbers. Even those who stay are often disappointed with what they are getting and carry on a sort of independent spiritual quest.

I have no particular interest in defending organized religion. It certainly has its problems. But when we feel ready to throw something away, it is wise to reflect for a moment on why it exists. It probably came to be for a reason and may still serve a purpose. The vision this book sketches for a man's life constitutes quite a stretch for most of us. Who can do it? It demands a change of heart and the deliberate cultivation of quite an exacting set of habits. We are lazy. We are cowardly. We sometimes start good projects—and then backslide. And the surrounding culture scarcely supports our higher aspirations. Is a man likely to succeed at being a really good man, and sustaining that through the years, all by himself?

That is where organized religion comes in, and perhaps here lies the heart of its purpose. It is stimulus, structure, and safety net. A very focused support structure relevant to the purpose of this book is a men's group. It serves the same purpose: stimulus, structure, and safety net. Let us consider the larger framework first, then the smaller.

Organized religion certainly has its faults but it does possess rich resources for teaching, nurturing, and supporting the spiritual life. For one thing, organized religion is human community, and that means very welcome support on an arduous trek. Religion also has a wealth of texts, eminent models, rituals, symbols, methods of prayer and meditation, trained leaders and guides, holy days and seasons, fruitful disciplines, and retreat opportunities, all in support of the kind of life it inculcates. In short, it has a lot of experience and a wealth of means, and so constitutes a stable, fruitful framework for spirituality's nurturance. One can go it alone in the spiritual life, but such a spurning of both community and experience can so easily lead to painful, wasteful misadventures, and before long to all loss of heart for the great adventure of the Spirit. At the very least, organized religion keeps our ideals before us, ever reorienting us amid life's changing currents, keeping us stretching in the right direction.

A priest friend of mine who married and so lost his clerical status told me how he still went to church most Sundays. His wife and children did not usually go with him. He admitted that the preaching was usually pretty bad, and much of the ritual held little meaning for him anymore. But the church building was sacred space, and it brought him into contact with the Presence. Gathered around him, he said, was a motley lot of fellow stragglers—there, like himself, to draw sustenance to keep on plodding in the right direction. It is a good place for me to be, he said. I pray, and I think about my life, and I get reoriented. I haven't been able to find another place or time to do that.

Men's groups do not all meet in churches, nor need they. But many do. And, like organized religion, men's groups constitute a structure for encouraging and supporting personal growth. Many who work with men today emphasize the need for men's groups as the crucial setting for real progress. A man usually needs the encouragement of other men, even their permission, before he can let his feelings rise to consciousness and expression. He also needs their understanding and support over time as he strives to master his sex drive, his aggressive impulses, and his anger. He probably needs a setting in which he can grieve some of what he has suffered or is suffering now. Men prove to have a lot to share with other men once the door opens a crack, deep things they have never shared with anyone. From here they can move on to other sharings. The group is often the place where men begin to find liberation from the many things that bind them. Also, men with more experience can be helpful to younger men in many areas of life, not least in relating more effectively to spouse and children. Many churches now sponsor these groups. More could help by taking up the cause.

If you cannot find a men's group, or do not wish to join one, you might find many of its benefits in a relationship with just one other man who wants to grow in the same ways that you do.

But why live a spiritual life, religious or otherwise, in the first place? The main reason, it seems, is that something very deep in us wants it, and wants it more than we want anything else. Spirituality gives meaning and direction to our lives, and we long for both. It supplies us with a compelling vision, daunting but attractive. It answers to our desire for a larger purpose, for something grand, ennobling, even heroic to give our little lives to. And it empowers us, helping us to do what we cannot do on our own.

To make clearer this vision of a wider horizon, let me share a brief portrait of the spiritual life created on the grid of an alphabetical list by two contemporary spiritual writers.

A— Attention
B— Being Present
C— Compassion
D— Devotion
E— Enthusiasm
F— Faith/Forgiveness
G— Grace/Gratitude
H— Hope/Hospitality
I— Imagination
J— Joy/Justice
K— Kindness
L— Listening/Love
M— Meaning
N— Nurturing
O— Openness
P— Peace/Play
Q— Questing
R— Reverence
S— Shadow/Silence
T— Transformation
U— Unity
V— Vision
W— Wonder
X— The Mystery
Y— Yearning/You
Z— Zeal

Spend just a moment with each of these items, and notice its appeal. There is a richness in these qualities, attitudes, and practices that calls to something deep in us. It sketches the sort of person we most admire and would ourselves like to be. Who does not want to be attentive? Compassionate? Grateful? Hopeful? Who does not want to listen and to love? To enjoy peace? To stand before the ordinary with a sense of wonder? When we contemplate a summary of habits like these, we recognize in them our highest possible development as persons. Not that achieving it is easy. It requires years of practice. But the same is true of other worthwhile human endeavors, even those of ultimately lesser importance, such as becoming a good athlete or businessman or musician or scholar. This list has to do with the kind of *person* we will be. And it is countercultural. It is not what most people put first in life. It diverges sharply from the pursuit of physical beauty, pleasure, riches, power, far more commonly the objects of human striving than the life of the Spirit. But it is clear that the best things in life are here, not in the preoccupations of popular culture.

You can throw away religion if it offends you, though this is risky. But if you cast off spirituality, you throw away your personal core.

A Model for Our Manhood?

Among the assets of organized religion are its exemplars, the great men and women who have been filled with Spirit and begun the movements that crystallized into the world's great religions. In these models we can see the spiritual life's two principal features. Whether we reflect on the life of Lao Tsu, Siddhartha Gautama, Moses, Jesus, or Muhammed (Taoism, Buddhism, Judaism, Christianity, Islam), we can discern, with variations, both a strong concern for personal wholeness and a sense of mission to the wider world. We also discover a grounding in a lived relationship with Mystery, as each understands it. They are aligned with it and teach us how to align ourselves with it. Rooted and grounded in that source, they dedicate themselves both to being the best persons they can be and to improving the lot of others. Each demonstrates that when we catch the Spirit, our greatest concern becomes the suffering of the world, our greatest yearning the healing of that world.

The spiritual giant familiar to most of us is Jesus, first-century Palestinian Jew. And while to some, conjuring up his memory at this point might seem a sharp detour from this book's interest, on closer examination he might just prove to be a useful model for us in our search for what it means to be a man. Not that any of us is Jesus, or could do what he did. But might we at least catch from him an orientation, if we take a closer look at what he was up to? Might we be able to translate that for our own circumstances and tailor it to the scope of our own abilities? Let us consider for a moment the broad outlines of his life in this light.

What strikes us first about the life of Jesus is how generously he lives it for other people. Open the gospels to any page, and you will find him doing something for someone. He welcomes and encourages, frees people from what burdens them, forgives their offenses, heals their diseases, feeds the hungry, and teaches wisdom. He shows a special outreach to society's "losers." And he courageously confronts the wealthy and powerful for creating the conditions that grind so many people down.

At the heart of Jesus' dedication to others is his vital relationship with the Mystery. It shows in many ways. He prays. He speaks familiarly of God in his teachings. He speaks and acts like a man on a mission, his passion to do the will of the One who "sent" him, to accomplish God's work. For him, the Mystery is clearly personal and loving besides. He calls the Mystery "Father," at times using an even more familiar term: "Abba," or "Papa." The God he knows, and reflects in his relationships with others, is a God compassionate, gracious, and faithful to human beings.

Jesus offers a simple summary of his entire teaching in his nation's capital near the end of his life. Answering a question as to which of God's commandments is the greatest, he says:

> "The first is, 'Hear, O Israel, the Lord our God is one God, and you must love the Lord your God with your whole heart and with your whole soul and with your whole mind and with your whole strength.' The second is this, 'You must love your neighbor as yourself.'" (Mark 12:30–31)

He quotes his people's scriptures here, but gives them a new twist. He intertwines the two parts of this one commandment, so that the criterion for the authenticity of our love of God is the way we relate to our fellow human beings.

The life of Jesus ends in violence, and it is little wonder. He challenges the established order, and the powerful see to his destruction. There is a parallel here with the endings of such people as Mohandas Gandhi and Martin Luther King, Jr. Jesus challenges the reigning religious authorities for legalistically laying burdens on people and not lifting a finger to help, for consuming the substance of widows, for fasting and giving alms in public mainly to impress, for preferring strict observance in tiny matters of law to the larger requirements of justice and mercy. He accuses them of murdering the persons God has sent from time to time to call them to their senses. In a symbolic gesture, he cuts them to the quick. He makes public protest against the commerce going on in the temple precincts. He offends them further with his outrageous demand that the rich give up their surplus to relieve the sufferings of the poor. Like that of spiritual persons before him and since, Jesus' theology is political. His dedication is to a radically transformed social order. And so he attracts a great following. Deeply threatened, both the Jewish and the Roman authorities of the time resolve to do away with him, and have him arrested and brought to trial. They charge him with stirring up the people, opposing the tribute to Caesar, and making himself a king. They crucify him.

This is the briefest sketch of the life of Jesus. Its proportions are heroic, and we feel totally outscaled. Here, I am interested in his values as a cue for our aspirations as men—his alignment with the Mystery, his obvious concern for other people, his way of being a man in the world. Who would question his virility—his clearheadedness, courage, or sense of purpose? He is a person to be reckoned with when justice is at stake. Yet what a model of compassion and gentleness he also is, what profound respect he shows for women as men's equals, what a warm heart he has for children. He feels deeply, and he shares those feelings. He is passionate about the well-being of all. He expresses anger on many occasions about the things he sees. Perhaps we can recognize in these broad outlines something of what it means to be a man.

Making a Start

So, having considered all this, what are some simple, concrete steps you could take starting today toward being a better man?

1. Begin by trying to recover your life of feeling. Use those probes suggested in Chapter 2 to rediscover what is going on inside you. Take a chance with someone you trust, and share some part of your personal self that you have never shared before.
2. Examine yourself for aggression, anger, and sexual exploitation. If you find yourself out of order, make a choice to tame these energies and put them in the service of what is good. If anger is habitual in your life, look under it for unhealed hurts, low-level depression, or unrecognized fears, and address those underlying issues.
3. If you are in a committed relationship, married or not, view it as a school in which you are given the opportunity to learn how to love. Choose one of the suggestions

enumerated in Chapter 6 and see if you can improve your behavior there.

4. If you are a dad, take a look at the way you are relating to your kids, and choose one of the areas laid out in Chapter 7 for improving something in your relationship to each child.
5. Take a walk or sit in some quiet place by yourself for a few hours the first opportunity you can get, and reflect on whether you are living out of your personal center or if you are caught up in some other program. Don't try to change everything at once, but choose one change you want to make and figure out how to bring it about.
6. Take a look at your working life, and ask if you are doing the work you want to be doing. If not, how can you make a transition? In either case, what is a single change that you would like to make in the way you go about your work to express more of your spirituality in it?
7. Reflect on your relationship to the women in your life, and on the state of women in the world at large. How would you like to alter the way you think about and relate to women? Is there something you could do to relieve women's oppression or empower women in the world?
8. Is there a gay man or lesbian woman in your acquaintance? Would you be willing to reach out and get to know that person a little better, so that you can begin to see the world from where they are?
9. Is there any spiritual practice—meditation, reading, a support group—that you would like to put in place to support your new orientation? Would you like to deepen your relationship with the Mystery by practicing some form of prayer?

And so this long trail of words comes to an end, with you and me both still working at becoming the men we aspire to be.

The endeavor will take us the rest of our lives, and our best moves will show the taint of imperfection. But we plod on. As G. K. Chesterton once remarked, whatever is worth doing is worth doing badly. A little parable from the wisdom tradition offers encouragement.

> One day the King of Persia was riding down the road on his camel when he came upon a sparrow lying on its back in the road, its feet pointed up into the air. The king stopped and looked at him. "Why are you lying in the road with your feet in the air?" he asked. "I heard the sky is going to fall today," the sparrow said solemnly. "And you think you can hold up the sky with your two puny little legs?" the king asked. The sparrow drew a deep breath and said quietly, "One does what one can."

Reading Suggestions

I am indebted to a talk that Jesuit Father Steve Sundborg gave at Seattle University for his thumbnail description of spirituality as "our lived relationship with Mystery."

The alphabetical list of the qualities of spiritual living comes from Frederic and Mary Ann Brussat, *Spiritual Literacy: Reading the Sacred in Everyday Life* (New York: Scribners, 1996), 28–29.

In my book *Spiritual Quest: A Guide to the Changing Landscape* (Mahwah, NJ: Paulist Press, 1999), I write much more extensively about what constitutes spirituality, how it relates to religion, how we can know whether our spirituality is authentic or not, and how we can grow spiritually. I offer fresh ways of thinking about God, Jesus, sexuality, and spirituality. The book is designed for people raised in the mainline Christian churches, dissatisfied with what they are finding there, and looking for guidance in the spiritual life.

Richard Rohr, *Quest for the Holy Grail* (New York: Crossroad, 1997), develops a spirituality for men based on the legends of the search for the Holy Grail.

Psychiatrist Joseph Novello, *The Myth of More* (Mahwah, NJ: Paulist Press, 2000), combines psychological and spiritual insights in a book promoting healing and wholeness.

Patton Boyle, Episcopal priest and therapist, blends Christian and shamanic insights into an attractive spiritual vision in his *Screaming Hawk: Flying Eagle's Training of a Mystic Warrior* (Barrytown, NY: Station Hill Press, 1994).

In Antony Fernando with Leonard Swidler, *Buddhism Made Plain: An Introduction for Christians and Jews* (Maryknoll, NY: Orbis Books, 1981), a Buddhist scholar who is a Christian (Fernando) and a Jewish scholar active in the Christian/Jewish dialogue (Swidler), combine their understandings to show the inner affinity of Buddhism, Judaism, and Christianity. It lies in the desire of each religion's founder to create a transformed human society *in this world.* Strangely, in the case of each of these religions, the founders' original project is transformed into a mainly otherworldly vision by their followers.

For more on how men's groups can support our efforts to grow as persons, see Frederick Grosse, *The Eight Masks of Men* (New York: Haworth, 1998). Terrence Real, *I Don't Want to Talk about It: Overcoming the Secret Legacy of Male Depression* (New York: Simon & Schuster, 1997), shows how a therapist leads men in groups toward the recovery of feeling and the healing of memories.

QUESTIONS FOR MEN'S GROUPS

1. Healing Boyhood Wounds

1. What are some of the early messages you received about what it means to be a man?
2. What teasing and nicknames do you remember receiving as a boy? What do you remember being done to you or by you that you would classify as cruel or hurtful?
3. What did it mean to be a man in college? In the military? At your first job or two?

2. Recovering Your World of Feeling

1. What kind of relationship did you have with your father, and how do you feel about it now?
2. What memories of specific interactions with your father stand out for you, and how do you feel about them?
3. What do you wish you had gotten from your father that he did not give you?
4. Have you ever been criticized for not sharing very much of yourself? What happens inside you when you hear that criticism?
5. Would you be willing to pick one member of this group, and go off with him for a few minutes to share something personal that you rarely or never share with anyone?

6. Would you be willing to share something personal with the whole group, maybe not of the same magnitude, yet something that would leave you feeling somewhat vulnerable?
7. Can you relate to what this chapter says about how anger is often a cover for fear, sadness, or hurt? Can you imagine yourself speaking of that underlying fear, sadness, or hurt with the person involved?

3. Mastering Anger and Violence

1. Do you see anger and violence as a problem for some other men, or as an issue that concerns you personally?
2. How can you bridle your anger and violence without becoming weak and being taken advantage of?
3. Would you be willing to eliminate violence in your business practices, driving, relationships with women and children (including verbal violence)? Would you be willing to do anything publicly to reduce violence against women, children, or animals?
4. Do you think you might be one of those men afflicted with low-level depression?

4. Putting Sex and Love Together

1. What were the early messages you received from family, church, or school about sexuality? How do you think about sexuality now?
2. Can you relate to what the chapter says about the deeper meaning of your sex drive and your loneliness?
3. Do you think your sexual relating needs some norms or guiding principles? If so, what are your norms?

4. What are some signs of true love between a man and a woman? What does sex have to do with it?

5. Looking for a Mate

1. What did you learn, or are you learning, from your search for a mate? Or have you chosen to remain single, at least for now?
2. Which of the fears named here do you most relate to: unworthiness, intimacy, commitment? Might the group have some helpful feedback for you?
3. Which of the common mistakes named here do you relate to personally? Are there other mistakes that come to mind?
4. If you have sought a mate without finding one, and if you never find one, what will your life be? Would you like to get the group's feedback on your answer to this?
5. Do you have any close men friends? Are they men you can open your heart to? Is there anything you could do to improve the quality of your male friendships?

6. Living a Committed Relationship

1. Choose two of your mate's habitual complaints about you, and explore with the group how you might address them.
2. Choose two of your frustrations with your mate, and reflect with the group on how you might address those.
3. Choose two of the nine suggestions made in the chapter, share with the group why they catch your attention, and explore how you might go about living them more fully. Do you see any spirituality involved here?

4. How do you think your marriage has changed you so far? How has it changed your mate?

7. Being a Dad

1. If you have children, how do you think being a dad has changed you?
2. What do you think of the idea of being coparent, as fully responsible for the raising of your kids as your wife is?
3. If being a model of what you want to inculcate is important, how do you feel called to personal growth by reason of your children?
4. Where do you stand on forming your son(s) to be the kind of men this book sees as the goal? How do you go about the task?
5. What experiences have you had caring for aging parents? Are you satisfied with the role you are playing?

8. Finding Your True Self

1. What ideas in this chapter spoke to you?
2. Are you living the life you want to be living? Are there changes you would like to make?
3. Would you be willing to try the inner probe, seeking to answer the four questions: What do I feel, think, need, and want, right now in this group?
4. Have you ever felt in your body the difference between a "should" and a "want" as motive for your behavior? Do you think it is safe for a man to live by his wants?
5. Do you think the idea is valid that when we have found what we most deeply want we have found God's will for us?

9. Taking Your Place in the World

1. How do you feel about your work?
2. Does your mate ever complain that your work takes up too much of your time and attention? What do you think?
3. Do any of the ideas presented here for living your spirituality in the work place appeal to you?
4. Do you think your work has any value beyond the money it pays you? What is that value?
5. What calls for reform in your business or profession to make it more just and ecologically sensitive?

10. Understanding Homophobia

1. Did you learn anything from this chapter?
2. What sorts of interaction have you had with gay men or lesbian women?
3. If you feel contempt or hatred of gay men or lesbian women, can you say why you feel that way? Does this chapter's naming of reasons have any validity for you personally?
4. If you have become empathic and supportive of gay men and lesbian women, how did you come to this attitude?
5. If you wanted to become empathic and supportive, how could you go about it?

11. Righting the Balance with Women

1. Do you agree or disagree that there is a fundamental injustice in the social system in the relative positions of men and women?

2. If you think there is an injustice, what are you doing or would you be willing to do to correct it, in relating to women yourself, and in addressing social structures on which you might have some influence?
3. Do the chapter's five items women would like from men strike you as fair and appropriate? What do these items ask of you personally?
4. Do you agree that religion has been part of the problem in women's oppression? Can it be part of the solution?
5. How important do you think this issue of sexism is?

12. Living Your Life Spiritually

1. Do you agree that this whole book has been about spirituality? If so, how?
2. Do you see any place for organized religion in your life? For prayer?
3. Do you agree that spirituality is something we want, something worth pursuing for its own rewards? You might look at the chapter's definition of spirituality, or the alphabetical list, as you ponder this question.
4. Do you think Jesus is a suitable model for what it means to be a man in today's world?
5. If you were to choose an item or two from the chapter's end as a place to begin some work on your own growth, what would those items be and why?